HOLT

Decisions for Health
LEVEL GREEN

Study Guide

HOLT, RINEHART AND WINSTON
A Harcourt Education Company

Orlando • **Austin** • New York • San Diego • Toronto • London

TO THE STUDENT

This Study Guide contains Concept Review worksheets, Health Inventories, Health Behavior Contracts, and Life Skills Activities. The Concept Review worksheets can be used as a pre-reading guide to help you identify the main concepts of each chapter before your initial reading. You can also use the worksheets after reading each chapter to test your understanding of the chapter's main concepts and terminology and to prepare for exams. Health Inventories can help you assess your own health and your knowledge of health topics. Life Skills Activities will allow you to practice the Life Skills. Regardless of how you and your teacher use *Decisions for Health Study Guide*, it will help you determine which topics you have learned well and which topics you need to study further.

ISBN-13: 978-0-03-099993-2
ISBN-10: 0-03-099993-6
03 04 05 0982 11 10 09

Contents

Friends and Family

Coping with Conflict and Stress

Caring for Your Body

Your Body Systems

Growth and Development

Controlling Disease

Physical Fitness

Nutrition

Understanding Drugs

Tobacco and Alcohol

Health and Your Safety

Skills Worksheet

Concept Review

Lesson: What Is Health?

In the blanks provided, write *PH* beside the examples of physical health, *EH* beside examples of emotional health, *MH* for mental health, and *SH* for social health.

_____ **1.** You take a shower every morning before school.

_____ **2.** You are considerate and try never to hurt the feelings of your friends.

_____ **3.** You exercise three or more times a week.

_____ **4.** You accept both your strengths and weakness.

_____ **5.** You adjust easily to your new class schedule for second semester.

_____ **6.** You always show up on time for your babysitting job.

_____ **7.** You are willing to try the new basketball drills that your coach introduces.

_____ **8.** You ask for help to deal with your sadness when your best friend moves out of state.

_____ **9**. You stay away from drugs and alcohol.

_____**10**. You support your friend when she refuses the offer of a cigarette.

11. How do the four parts of health affect your wellness?

_____

_____

_____

12. Why do you think it is important to start taking care of your health when you are young?

_____

_____

_____

Lesson: What Influences Your Health?

In the blanks provided, define each of the following terms.

13. heredity

_____

14. environment

_____

Complete each item below.

15. How do traits relate to heredity? Give an example.

_____

_____

16. How does heredity affect your health?

_____

_____

_____

17. Identify at least three elements of the environment that can affect your health. Can you control any of these elements? To what extent? Explain.

_____

_____

_____

_____

Lesson: Healthy Attitudes

In the blanks provided, define each of the following terms.

18. lifestyle

_____

_____

❙ Concept Review *continued*

19. attitude

_____

_____

20. List three examples of preventive health care.

_____

_____

_____

21. What part does lifestyle play in determining your overall health?

_____

_____

_____

22. To what extent do you have control over your health? Explain.

_____

_____

_____

_____

23. Give at least two examples of responsible choices you can make to improve your health.

_____

_____

_____

Lesson: Life Skills to Improve Your Health

Identify the life skill that is illustrated in each of the following situations.

24. Sonia has a problem she can't figure out, so she asks her mother for advice.

_____

25. Cary and Manny talk out their differences instead of holding grudges.

_____

26. To earn her brown belt, Tess plans to practice karate four times a week.

_____

27. Jamal turns down an invitation to a party where alcohol will be available.

_____

28. Products advertised on TV are not necessarily the ones Karen buys.

_____

29. Lee gets plenty of sleep every night and eats a balanced diet.

_____

30. At the sports store, Juan compares the quality of two jerseys before buying.

_____

31. Liz decides to put in an extra half hour of study the night before her test.

_____

32. Aaron periodically takes time to evaluate his health habits.

_____

33. List four ways that life skills can help you.

_____

_____

_____

_____

Name _____ Class _____ Date _____

Life Skills: Practicing Wellness

Lesson: What Is Health?

PLANNING A BALANCED DIET

Follow these steps to create and carry out a balanced diet for a day.

1. Review what you know about eating a balanced diet. You can find a copy of the recommended food pyramid in your health book, in the health office at school, at your doctor's office, or in a current encyclopedia.

2. Plan a menu for yourself for one day. Be sure to include the recommended number of servings for each food group. Try to balance your food intake throughout the day.

3. Use the chart below to plan and record your menu.

Breakfast	Lunch	Dinner	Snacks

4. Use this second chart to record what you actually ate.

Breakfast	Lunch	Dinner	Snacks

Life Skills *continued*

Now, answer these questions about your menu planning.

1. Was your food plan balanced according to the requirements of the food pyramid? Explain.

_____

_____

_____

_____

2. How does the record of what you actually ate differ from your original plan?

_____

_____

_____

_____

3. In what areas is your present diet lacking? Do you need to eat more fruits and vegetables? Are you getting enough protein? Too much fat or sugar?

_____

_____

_____

_____

4. If you were to make one change to make your diet, and yourself, healthier, what would it be? Why would this change be important?

_____

_____

_____

_____

_____

_____

Activity

Life Skills: Coping

Lesson: Life Skills to Improve Your Health
MANAGING STRESS

Read the following situation. Then answer the questions in the spaces provided.

Carey's family moved across country in the middle of the school year. She finds herself trying to adjust to a new house, neighborhood, and school. She misses the familiarity and comfort of her old home and school and feels that she is not fitting in here—especially at school. The textbooks are different, she doesn't know the teachers, and the kids all dress and talk differently than she is used to. Carey responds by trying to be "invisible" in class and saying as little as possible. She is not happy at all and is feeling very stressed.

1. What factors are causing Carey stress?

_____

_____

2. What does Carey do to cope with her new situation?

_____

_____

3. Brainstorm some ways that Carey might better deal with her stress and become more accepting of her new home.

_____

_____

_____

4. How might Carey's classmates help her make the transition to her new school?

_____

_____

_____

_____

Name _____ Class _____ Date _____

Concept Review

Lesson: You Are a Decision Maker!

1. Describe what a good decision is.

_____

2. List three things that influence decision making.

_____

_____

_____

3. A(n) _____ is the result of an action you take.

Match each definition with the correct term. Write the letter in the space provided.

_____ **4.** consequences that help you or other people

_____ **5.** consequences that neither help nor hurt you or other people

_____ **6.** consequences that do harm to you or to other people

a. neutral
b. negative
c. positive

Lesson: Six Simple Steps to Good Decisions

Use the terms from the following list to complete the sentences below. Each term may be used only once. Some terms will not be used.

take a look at	problem	results
brainstorm	options	decision
values	consequences	goals

The first step in decision making is to identify the **7.** _____.

The next step is to think about how your **8.** _____ relate to

the problem. The third step is to list all of your **9.** _____,

or ways that you can handle the problem. One way to do this is to

10. _____ all of the possible ways to carry out your decision.

Next, consider the **11.** _____ of all of your options. Think

about which option will bring about the best **12.** _____ for

10

| Concept Review *continued*

you and for others. Once you have acted on a decision, you should stand back

and **13.** _____ your decision.

14. Thinking about the consequences of your choices will help you to make

_____.

15. Describe how values influence your decisions.

_____

_____

_____

Lesson: Facing Pressure

Write the letter of the correct answer in the space provided.

_____**16.** The feeling that you should do something because your friends want
you to is called
   a. excitement.
   b. peer pressure.
   c. anger.
   d. fear.

_____**17.** Positive peer pressure can help you make good decisions, while nega-
tive peer pressure can keep you from
   a. doing the right thing.
   b. doing the wrong thing.
   c. making mistakes.
   d. None of the above

_____**18.** A refusal skill is a strategy you can use to do all of the following
EXCEPT
   a. handle negative peer pressure.
   b. stand your ground.
   c. avoid responsibility.
   d. avoid doing something yo don't want to do.

_____**19.** When friends pressure you to do something you don't want to do,
sometimes you need to act
   a. passively.
   b. aggressively.
   c. angrily.
   d. assertively.

20. List five refusal skills.

_____

_____

_____

_____

_____

21. How does having a support system help you?

_____

_____

Lesson: Goals

Write the letter of the correct answer in the space provided.

_____**22.** A goal that can take years to reach is called a
   a. short-term goal.
   b. long-term goal.
   c. immediate goal.
   d. quick goal.

23. Describe how setting and achieving goals can improve your feelings about yourself.

_____

_____

24. Describe one example of how having goals can improve your relationships with other people.

_____

_____

_____

_____

Name _____ Class _____ Date _____

| Concept Review *continued*

25. Define *success*.

_____

_____

Lesson: Choosing and Reaching Your Goals

In the blanks provided, fill in the letters of the term or phrase being described.

26. something that you enjoy and want to learn more about __ __ T __ __ __S __

27. something you use to help you   __ __ S __ __ R __ __

28. a person who can give you good advice   __ E __ __ O __

29. a step toward your goal   __ C __ O __ __ L __ __ __ M __ __ T

30. a prize you give yourself for accomplishing a task   R__ __ A __ D

Answer the following questions.

31. Describe how your interests and values can influence the goals you set.

_____

_____

_____

32. Name four resources that can help you reach your goals.

_____

_____

_____

_____

33. Name two rewards you could give yourself for accomplishing a step toward one of your goals.

_____

_____

_____

Name _____ Class _____ Date _____

Health Inventory

Making Good Decisions

Read each statement below. Decide whether it describes how you take responsibility for your decisions. Write *always, sometimes,* or *never* in the space to the left of each statement.

_____ **1.** I identify the problem that needs to be solved before making a decision.

_____ **2.** I seek reliable information before making important decisions.

_____ **3.** I base my decisions on knowledge, not emotions.

_____ **4.** I make many decisions by myself.

_____ **5.** I consider both the positive and negative consequences of my options.

_____ **6.** When making decisions, I recognize which factors are beyond my control and which are within my control.

_____ **7.** I apply the six-step decision-making process when I make decisions.

_____ **8.** I am aware that many of the decisions I make will lead to other decisions.

_____ **9.** I resist negative peer pressure when faced with difficult decisions.

_____ **10.** When considering decisions, I consider my values and goals.

Score yourself on this quiz. Give yourself 2 points for each *always* answer, 1 point for each *sometimes,* and 0 for each *never*. Write your score here _____.

15–20: Excellent—You always take responsibility for your decisions.
10–14: Good—You often take responsibility for your decisions.
5–9: Fair—You can improve your decision-making skills.
Less than 5: Poor—You need to work on building sound decision-making skills.

Name _____ Class _____ Date _____

Health Behavior Contract

Making Good Decisions

My Goals: I, _____, will accomplish one or more of the following goals:

I will use the six-step method for making decisions.

I will work toward one long-term goal.

I will practice at least one refusal skill.

Other: _____

_____

My Reasons: By using the six-step method of decision making, I will make better choices. I will also improve my ability to set short-term and long-term goals. By using refusal skills, I will make more-responsible decisions.

Other: _____

_____

My Values: Personal values that will help me meet my goals are

_____

_____

_____

My Plan: The actions I will take to meet my goals are

_____

_____

_____

Evaluation: I will use my Health Journal to keep a log of actions I took to fulfill this contract. After 1 month, I will evaluate my goals. I will adjust my plan if my goals are not being met. If my goals are being met, I will consider setting additional goals.

Signed _____

Date _____

Activity

Life Skills: Communicating Effectively

Lesson: Facing Pressure
BEING ASSERTIVE

Knowing how to communicate clearly and effectively is important to healthy relationships. By being able to communicate assertively, you have a greater chance of carrying out your decisions and reaching your goals. Consider the following situation:

Randy, Fred's best friend, has his birthday one week before Fred's. Randy has not made plans for his party yet and asks what Fred is planning to do for his birthday. Fred tells him that he is going to have a pizza party. Three days later, Fred receives an invitation to Randy's pizza party.

Follow these guidelines to help you communicate assertively.

1. **State the situation in a healthy way.** Describe the situation and identify how Fred may feel about it.

2. **Show understanding for the other person's point of view.** What is Randy's role in the situation? How is he feeling? Chances are that Randy is right in some way, and frustrated too.

3. **Explore a fair solution.** What might Fred like to see happen? What do you think Randy would like to see happen? Express how you think Fred is feeling and what he thinks is a fair solution. Let Randy do the same.

4. **Respond to the other person's reply.** How can Fred respond to Randy's questions and statements?

5. **Treat yourself and others with respect.** Do Fred's actions show respect for everyone involved?

Write down two ways that Fred could tell Randy how he feels.

_____

_____

_____

Write down two ways that Fred could resolve the situation fairly.

_____

_____

_____

Activity

Life Skills: Setting Goals

Lesson: Goals
CREATING A HEALTHY DIET

Your body needs a variety of food to stay healthy and to grow properly. It uses the vitamins and minerals in food in many ways. By eating a variety of foods and following the MyPyramid recommendations, you will be well on your way to good nutrition.

WHAT WILL I EAT TODAY?

Think about your height, weight, and your activity level, and plan a daily menu for yourself according to the MyPyramid recommendations. (Refer to the chapter in your textbook about nutrition if necessary.)

_____

_____

_____

_____

_____

_____

| Life Skills *continued*

1. What are some new foods you could try so you would meet your daily food goals?

   _____

   _____

   _____

   _____

   _____

2. What are some goals you can set to make sure you include foods from every food group in your daily diet?

   _____

   _____

   _____

   _____

   _____

3. Why is eating a nutrient-rich diet important for good health?

   _____

   _____

   _____

   _____

   _____

4. What is one of your nutritional goals? What are some of the steps you can take to make sure you are successful in reaching your goal?

   _____

   _____

   _____

   _____

   _____

   _____

Name _____ Class _____ Date _____

Concept Review

Lesson: Self-Esteem and You

In the blanks provided, write *HSE* next to the scenario which encourages healthy self-esteem or *LSE* next to the scenario which fosters low self-esteem.

_____ **1.** You are proud of the perfect grades you get on tests. Today your teacher passed back the Chapter Test and you got a B+. You realize you could have done better, but are not mad at yourself.

_____ **2.** Even though most of your friends order burgers and pizza, you enjoy ordering salad because it's good for you and it makes you feel good to be an individual.

_____ **3.** You saw your friend whisper something to another classmate. You're sure they're making plans and you're not going to be invited to come along.

_____ **4.** At your ball game, you look over at the sidelines and don't see your parents. Usually they come and cheer, but they had an important meeting to attend and knew you'd be okay if they missed one game.

_____ **5.** After a haircut, someone says to you, "Did you have your ears lowered?" but you feel good about how you look, so you just smile.

_____ **6.** Your friends tell you that you look like a famous musician. You're not so sure you really do, but you appreciate the comparison and your friends' interest in you.

_____ **7.** You've stopped brushing your teeth in the morning because you can't stand looking in the mirror at your mouth full of braces and rubber bands.

_____ **8.** A group of guys are standing around smoking cigarettes, one of the group offers you one, you decline, one of them calls you a wimp. You laugh and respond, "Whatever."

_____ **9.** You are walking to class with your buddies, you trip in the hall, your buddies laugh, you laugh with them.

_____ **10.** You practiced for months to get on the team. Although you were not selected, you feel good about your effort and will try again next time.

11. Explain how the media can impact your level of self-esteem.

_____

_____

| **Concept Review** *continued* |

12. Media, by usually showing only very successful and attractive people, can

hurt your _____.

Lesson: Your Self-Concept

13. _____ is how you feel about yourself.

14. _____ is how you see and imagine yourself.

15. How you see yourself as a student is called your _____.

16. How you see your physical abilities is called your _____.

17. How you see yourself in relationships is called your _____.

18. A _____ self-concept may lead to an unhealthy level of

self-esteem.

Match the area of self concept with the appropriate name. Use the letters *AS* (academic), *PS* (physical), and *SS* (social) to identify the specific area of self-concept.

_____ **19.** son/daughter

_____ **20.** student

_____ **21.** cheerleader

_____ **22.** brother

_____ **23.** swimmer

Lesson: Building Self-Esteem

24. List three key ways to build healthy self-esteem.

_____

_____

_____

25. Taking responsibility for your actions is called _____.

26. Acting on your thoughts and values with respect and honesty is called being

_____.

27. Knowing what is right and wrong is a way to _____

yourself.

Concept Review *continued*

---

28. By knowing yourself, you can build healthy self-esteem. Knowing yourself

means understanding what your _____ and your

_____ are.

29. You can help people who need help by _____ your time,
effort, and energy.

30. Identify five ways to build healthy self-esteem.

_____

_____

_____

_____

_____

Fill in the blanks with the appropriate letters to complete the words in 31–33

31. A way to healthy self-esteem that means being comfortable with your

appearance is __ C __ __ __ __ __ __ G yourself.

32. A way to healthy self-esteem that means following a plan for a certain

achievement called is __ __ T __ __ __ __ a goal.

33. A way to healthy self-esteem that means being your own personal cheerleader

is __ __ __ N G   __ O __ __ T __ __ __.

Name _____ Class _____ Date _____

Health Inventory

Self-Esteem

Use the following questions to help you evaluate your level of self-esteem.

yes	no		
❏	❏	**1.** I value, respect, and feel confident about myself.	40 points
❏	❏	**2.** I like the way I look.	15 points
❏	❏	**3.** I am comfortable with my body weight.	10 points
❏	❏	**4.** My friends are very supportive of me.	8 points
❏	❏	**5.** I rarely get upset with members of my family.	5 points
❏	❏	**6.** I am comfortable with my strengths and weaknesses and feel positive about myself, most of the time.	5 points
❏	❏	**7.** I see my body as normal and I am comfortable with it.	8 points
❏	❏	**8.** I see myself being exceptional at something some day.	5 points
❏	❏	**9.** As I grow emotionally, my self-concept will evolve.	3 points
❏	❏	**10.** I know that I must work at improving my self-esteem.	10 points

Add up the points for all of the questions to which you answered yes. Write your score here _____ .

Look at the scale to see how your level of self-esteem matches up. Remember, a scale like this is only one way to evaluate your level of self-esteem, so do not put a great deal of emphasis on a single measure.

40–109 points: You are the most comfortable with who you are and where you are going. keep up he great work.

20–39 points: You feel pretty good about yourself but you still have some negative, stressful times

15-19 points: You are balancing between positive self-esteem and not so positive self-esteem. Look for more positive opportunities.

0-14 points: Your self-esteem appears low and could use a big boost.

Name _____ Class _____ Date _____

Health Behavior Contract

Self-Esteem

My goals: I, _____, will accomplish one or more of the following goals:

I will build a higher self-esteem.

I will focus on my strengths.

I will make a plan to improve my weaknesses.

Other: _____

_____

My reasons: By building healthy self-esteem, I will improve my overall confidence and attitude, and I will feel good about myself as a person.

Other: _____

_____

My values: Personal values that will help me meet my goals are

_____

_____

_____

My plan: The actions I will take to meet my goals are

_____

_____

_____

Evaluation: I will use my Health Journal to keep a log of actions I took to fulfill this contract. After one month, I will evaluate my goals. I will adjust my plan if my goals are not being met. If my goals are being met, I will consider setting additional goals.

Signed _____

Date _____

Name _____ Class _____ Date _____

Life Skills: Communicating Effectively

Lesson: Self-Esteem and You
SELF-TALK: COMMUNICATING WITH YOURSELF

1. Situations often arise that make us feel stupid or clumsy. It may be that we dropped our books in the hallway, tripped going up the steps, or had some of this morning's breakfast still in our teeth. Situations like these happen to everyone at one time or another. Regardless, we still feel embarrassed. Identify your most recent embarrassing moment.

_____

_____

_____

2. When this embarrassing situation happened, what did you say to yourself? Many times people are really hard on themselves saying things like, "You dummy," "What an idiot I am," and "I am such a freak." Negative self-talk lowers our level of self-esteem. What if we responded by laughing at the situation and talking to ourselves in a positive way? Describe how you could have reacted to your most recent embarrassing moment using positive self-talk.

_____

_____

_____

Write down a positive response to the potentially embarrassing situations presented below.

1. You trip going up the steps.

_____

_____

2. You discover part of your lunch in your teeth.

_____

_____

3. You drop your books in the hall.

_____

_____

Name _____ Class _____ Date _____

Life Skills: Setting Goals

Lesson: Building Self-Esteem
SETTING GOALS TO GUIDE US

If you do not know where you're going, any road will take you there. You may have heard this before. It not only applies to a journey in the car, but to your quest for success as well. It has been said that "life is a journey," so if you want to achieve certain goals, then you must plan your trip. You may want to be a star athlete, an excellent student, or a terrific musician. To achieve these goals, you must plan your journey. First of all, you need to decide a few things.

In the space provided answer the questions about your "journey."

1. As the old saying goes, "What do you want to be when you grow up?"

_____

_____

2. Identify three people who currently have the kind of position you identified above. They can be people you know, people you have seen in the media, or someone you have only heard about.

_____

_____

_____

3. List three characteristics that each of the people listed above have. Such characteristics might include being funny, honest, trusting, loving, or any other characteristic. If you're not sure, then identify characteristics you feel they probably have.

a1 _____ b1 _____ c1 _____

a2 _____ b2 _____ c2 _____

a3 _____ b3 _____ c3 _____

4. Which characteristics did any of the people share?

_____

_____

_____

Life Skills: Setting Goals *continued*

5. Are all the characteristics listed important to developing positive self-esteem? Place a check mark next to the characteristics in question 3 that help develop positive self-esteem. Place an X next to the characteristics in question 3 that you think you currently have.

6. Explain why you think that you have the characteristics you placed an X next to.

_____

_____

_____

7. Write down ways you could develop the characteristics you did not place an X next to (hint: the seven ways to healthy self-esteem may be helpful).

_____

_____

_____

_____

_____

_____

8. Describe how these characteristics would help you along the road to success.

_____

_____

_____

_____

Skills Worksheet

Concept Review

Lesson: An Image of Yourself

1. What does *body image* mean?

_____

_____

_____

2. What is a benefit of feeling comfortable with your body?

_____

_____

_____

3. What is a drawback of not feeling comfortable with your body?

_____

_____

_____

Read each of the phrases below. If a phrase refers to a healthy body image, write H in the blank. If a phrase refers to an unhealthy body image, write U.

_____ **4.** fad dieting

_____ **5.** high self-esteem

_____ **6.** unhealthy behaviors

_____ **7.** avoiding friends

_____ **8.** eating disorders

_____ **9.** comfortable with appearance

_____**10.** accepting one's appearance

_____**11.** becoming less active

_____**12.** confident

_____**13.** easily influenced by others

Name _____ Class _____ Date _____

| Concept Review continued

Lesson: Influences on Body Image

Use the terms from the following list to complete the sentences below. Each item may be used only once.

body image   unrealistic   family
typical   thin   muscular
physical characteristics

14. Right now, your _____ may be the largest influence on your body image.

15. Your friends can be good influences on your _____ if they support you when you feel uncomfortable with your body.

16. Teens on TV are not _____.

17. The images of teens shown in magazines are often _____.

18. The girls shown in magazines and on TV are often _____.

19. The boys shown in magazines and on TV are often _____.

20. Your _____ may affect how well you play in a sport.

21. Name two ways that peers can affect your body image in a negative way.

_____

_____

_____

_____

_____

22. How can friends help you build a healthy body image?

_____

_____

_____

_____

_____

Copyright © by Holt, Rinehart and Winston. All rights reserved.

Decisions for Health   **28**   Body Image

Lesson: Building a Healthy Body Image

In the blanks provided, fill in the missing letters of the terms being described.

23. a factor in determining how you look

e _ h _ _ c _ _ y

24. a tool to help you find your healthy weight range (3 words)

_ o _ _   m _ s _   i _ _ e _

25. walking is an example of this type of activity

_ x e _ c i _ _

26. being honest with yourself about your potential

b _ _ n _   _ e _ l _ _ t _ _

27. helps you build a healthy body image (2 words)

g _ _ _   n _ t _ i t _ _ _

28. what healthy eating provides

e _ _ r _ y

29. Reena was the only one wearing jeans at a party because she thinks her legs have a funny shape. If Reena had had a better body image, what would she have done differently at the party?

_____

_____

_____

_____

30. How would you describe a "normal" teenager? Is there such a thing as "normal?"

_____

_____

_____

_____

Lesson: Eating Disorders

Use the terms from the following list to complete the sentences below. Each term may be used only once.

obese   behaviors   self-esteem
bulimia nervosa   eating disorder   anorexia nervosa
abuse

31. Some people feel so bad about their bodies that they develop unhealthy eating

_____.

32. Low _____ is one cause of eating disorders.

33. A(n) _____ is a disease in which a person is overly

concerned with his or her body weight and shape.

34. Some eating disorders are caused by sexual and physical

_____.

35. Symptoms of _____ include dry skin, brittle nails, and

hair loss.

36. People who suffer from _____ get rid of their food by

purging.

37. People who are _____ may develop high blood pressure

and heart problems.

Name _____ Class _____ Date _____

Health Inventory

Body Image

Read each statement below. Decide whether it describes your body image or your eating habits. Put a check next to each statement that describes you.

_____ **1.** I am comfortable with the way I look.

_____ **2.** I am not easily influenced by what people say about my appearance.

_____ **3.** I feel confident in new situations.

_____ **4.** I eat nutritious snack foods.

_____ **5.** I drink at least eight to ten glasses of water a day.

_____ **6.** I have fruits and vegetables with every meal.

_____ **7.** I never go on fad diets.

_____ **8.** I never skip meals.

_____ **9.** I have high self-esteem.

_____ **10.** I rarely compare myself with people I see on television.

_____ **11.** Negative comments from peers about my body don't bother me.

_____ **12.** I always stay within my healthy weight range.

Give yourself one point for each checkmark. Write your score here _____.

10–12:	Excellent—You have a healthy body image, and your eating habits support good nutrition.
6–9:	Good—You have some healthy habits, but some adjustments could help build a healthier body image.
Fewer than 6:	You may benefit from learning about nutrition, body image, and media influence.

Name _____ Class _____ Date _____

Health Behavior Contract

Body Image

My Goals: I, _____, will accomplish one or more of the following goals:

I will improve my body image.

I will avoid following unhealthy eating behaviors, such as fad dieting.

I will make healthy food choices.

I will be physically active every day.

Other: _____

_____

My Reasons: By building a healthy body image, I will be able to face new challenges with confidence and feel comfortable around my friends and peers. By making healthy food choices and being physically active, I will maintain a healthy weight.

Other: _____

_____

My Values: Personal values that will help me meet my goals are

_____

_____

_____

My Plan: The actions I will take to meet my goals are

_____

_____

_____

Evaluation: I will use my Health Journal to keep a log of actions I took to fulfill this contract. After 1 month, I will evaluate my goals. I will adjust my plan if my goals are not being met. If my goals are being met, I will consider setting additional goals.

Signed _____

Date _____

Activity

Life Skills: Evaluating Media Messages

Lesson: An Image of Yourself

ANALYZING ADS

Advertisements are written to sell products or services. Often, the product or service promises to change the buyer in a positive way. For example, the ad might promise to make you thinner or stronger. Some ads provide information about useful products. Other ads, however, may be misleading. They may promise something that would be impossible for the average person to achieve. Or they may contain information that is totally false. How can you tell which ads are telling the truth and which ones are not? You can better evaluate ads if you know about the major techniques that advertisers use to sell their products. Read the first two columns of the table below to familiarize yourself with major advertising techniques.

Locate three advertisements for health-related products or services in newspapers or magazines. Then, show the technique or techniques used in each ad by placing a check mark or marks in the appropriate boxes of the table on the next page. When you have completed the activity, answer the following question.

1. How can performing this activity help you identify true and false claims in advertisements?

   _____

   _____

   _____

   _____

   _____

   _____

Name _____ Class _____ Date _____

Life Skills continued

Advertising Technique	Association	Advertisement #1:	Advertisement #2:	Advertisement #3:
Information	facts about the product			
Status	associates product or service with people who are successful			
Peer approval	associates product or service with people in your age group			
Hero endorsement	associates use of product with a famous person			
Attraction	associates use of product with increased appeal to the opposite sex			
Entertainment	associates product with entertainment and feelings of enjoyment			
Intelligence	associates product with intelligent people, those who can't be fooled by inferior products or gimmicks			
Independence	associates product with people who are independent thinkers			

Name _____ Class _____ Date _____

Life Skills: Assessing Your Health

Lesson: Eating Disorders
RATING YOUR EATING PATTERNS

Answer the questions below to evaluate your eating behavior. Write the number of your answer on the blanks.

_____ **a.** How often do you diet?
  1. never   **3.** often
  2. rarely   **4.** always

_____ **b.** How often do you skip meals?
  1. never   **3.** often
  2. rarely   **4.** always

_____ **c.** What do you eat if you want a snack?
  1. fruit   **3.** bag of chips
  2. small sandwich **4.** donuts or pastry

_____ **d.** Do you take pills or supplements to gain or lose weight?
  1. never   **3.** often
  2. rarely   **4.** always

_____ **e.** Do you experience dry skin, brittle nails, and hair loss?
  1. rarely   **3.** often
  2. sometimes   **4.** all the time

_____ **f.** Do you stay within your healthy weight range?
  1. always   **3.** rarely
  2. often   **4.** never

_____ **g.** Do you eat normally in front of others and binge when you are alone?
  1. never   **3.** often
  2. rarely   **4.** always

Add up the numbers you have written in the blanks. Write your score here _____.

 7–14: Congratulations! You have very healthy eating habits.
15–21: Your eating habits could use improvement.
22–28: Your poor eating habits may be putting you in danger of harming
        your health.

Name _____ Class _____ Date _____

Concept Review

Lesson: Relationship Skills

Match the definitions with the correct term. Write the letter in the space provided.

_____ **1.** family

_____ **2.** relationship

_____ **3.** behavior

_____ **4.** empathy

_____ **5.** listening

_____ **6.** communication

_____ **7.** tolerance

a. how to choose to act

b. sending and receiving messages clearly

c. a social or emotional connection between people

d. paying attention to a speaker

e. a couple, with or without children or other relatives

f. putting differences aside and accepting people as they are

g. understanding and sharing another person's feelings

8. Family, friends, and teams are examples of groups of people who have a

_____ .

9. Paying attention to what someone is saying and looking at them is an example

of good _____ skills.

10. You are exhibiting _____ behavior if you do not speak up

when someone threatens your values and beliefs.

11. The way you look, the action of your hands, and the way you stand are part of

how your _____ is communicated.

12. When you are willing to listen to your friends' points of view, you are building

a stronger relationship with them by showing _____ .

| Concept Review *continued*

Lesson: Family Relationships

13. Complete the table below by filling in six ways that you can help your family function smoothly. Give an example of each.

Six ways to help my family function smoothly	Examples:

14. Explain why family members in different families perform different roles.

_____

_____

_____

15. What are three ways to show affection in a family?

_____

_____

_____

_____

| Concept Review *continued* |

16. How can you show support for your family?

_____

_____

_____

_____

17. How is a blended family different from an extended family?

_____

_____

_____

_____

_____

Lesson: Facing Family Problems

Place the steps of managing a minor family conflict in the order in which the steps should be taken. Place the numbers *1* to *4* next to the appropriate steps.

_____**18.** After everyone has spoken, identify the problem.

_____**19.** Allow each person in the conflict to tell his or her side of the story.

_____**20.** Allow time for each person in the conflict to calm down.

_____**21.** Try to find an answer everyone can agree on.

Match the first half of the sentence on the left with the second half of the sentence on the right. Write the letter of the correct response in the space provided.

_____**22.** Family meetings

_____**23.** Abuse and neglect

_____**24.** Victims of abuse and neglect

_____**25.** A family conflict

_____**26.** All families

_____**27.** Talking about family conflicts

a. go through times of change and difficulty.

b. can seek help from a trusted adult.

c. can help resolve family conflicts.

d. are always wrong.

e. is one of the best ways to cope with difficult changes.

f. is a clash of ideas or interests within a family.

Name _____ Class _____ Date _____

| Concept Review *continued*

Lesson: Friendship

28. What questions could you ask to determine whether someone would make a good friend for you?

_____

_____

_____

_____

_____

_____

_____

29. What questions can you ask to determine whether you are in a bad relationship?

_____

_____

_____

_____

30. Compare the benefits of positive peer pressure with the risks of negative peer pressure.

_____

_____

_____

_____

_____

_____

Lesson: Improving Friendships

Place the following terms next to the description of a behavior that demonstrates the term: *cooperation, support, friendship, respect, leadership,* **and** *popularity.*

31. Using refusal skills when someone wants you to smoke

_____

32. Working with someone to complete a project

_____

33. Encouraging your friends to stick to their values

_____

34. Being honest when you disagree with your friends

_____

35. Going along with everyone else so that they will like you

_____

36. Accepting the differences between you and your friends

_____

Lesson: Healthy Affection

37. What are five healthy ways to show affection?

_____

_____

_____

_____

_____

38. What are two benefits of practicing abstinence?

_____

_____

_____

_____

Name _____   Class _____   Date _____

Activity

Health Inventory

Friends and Family

Use the following questions to assess how healthy your behavior is in your family and friendships. Place a check on the appropriate line next to the question.

yes	no		
❏	❏	**1.** I feel comfortable talking to my parents about how I feel.	30 points
❏	❏	**2.** I listen to my family members and friends when they talk to me.	25 points
❏	❏	**3.** I am a good friend.	20 points
❏	❏	**4.** I use assertive behavior most of the time.	15 points
❏	❏	**5.** I can imagine or understand how others might feel.	15 points
❏	❏	**6.** I help my friends when they need it.	12 points
❏	❏	**7.** I tell my parents about problems that I see.	10 points
❏	❏	**8.** I would talk to an adult if there were a major problem in my family.	8 points
❏	❏	**9.** My body language always matches what I am saying.	6 points
❏	❏	**10.** I accept responsibility for my role in the family.	6 points
❏	❏	**11.** I never encourage my friends to go against their values.	5 points
❏	❏	**12.** I work well with others to get work done.	5 points
❏	❏	**13.** I can say no if someone tries to get me to do something wrong.	3 points
❏	❏	**14.** I respect myself and others.	3 points
❏	❏	**15.** I feel comfortable seeking help from others.	2 points

Add up all the points for the statements to which you answered yes. Use the scale below to see how you rate in the positive behavior you demonstrate to your friends and family.

SCALE	
120 to 165 points:	You have excellent communication skills and demonstrate positive behavior toward family and friends all of the time.
85 to 119 points:	You have very good communication skills and demonstrate positive behavior toward friends and family most of the time.
60 to 84 points:	You have good communication skills but you need to increase positive behavior toward family and friends.
0 to 59 points:	Improving your communication skills and increasing positive behavior with family and friends will help you build better relationships.

Name _____ Class _____ Date _____

Health Behavior Contract

Friends and Family

My Goals: I, _____, will accomplish one or more of the following goals:

I will support my family.

I will show leadership to my friends.

I will use my refusal skills.

Other: _____

_____

My Reasons: By improving my relationships, I will help support my family and friends. I can also develop leadership skills, learn better communication skills, and help keep myself safe and healthy.

Other: _____

_____

My Values: Personal values that will help me meet my goals are

_____

_____

_____

My Plan: The actions I will take to meet my goals are

_____

_____

_____

Evaluation: I will use my Health Journal to keep a log of actions I took to fulfill this contract. After 1 month, I will evaluate my goals. I will adjust my plan if my goals are not being met. If my goals are being met, I will consider setting additional goals.

Signed _____

Date _____

Activity

Life Skills: Communicating Effectively

Lesson: Relationship Skills
COMMUNICATING WITH FAMILY

You can learn to use your body language to help communicate with your family. Read the following situation. Then, answer the questions.

Susan has her head down on the table. When her mother asks her to come help with dinner, Susan looks up and frowns. Her mother asks her what is wrong. Susan shakes her head and says, "Nothing." Susan's mother wonders what is wrong with Susan and why she refuses to talk to her.

1. What emotion is Susan communicating with her head on the table?

_____

2. What body language does Susan use to communicate her feelings?

_____

_____

3. Why does Susan's mother ask her what is wrong?

_____

_____

4. What are the three ways that body language is used to communicate?

_____

_____

_____

5. How would you handle a situation when a person's words don't match his or her body language?

_____

_____

6. Describe how Susan's body language would change if she were feeling happy.

_____

7. What suggestions would you give to Susan to help her communicate better with her mother?

_____

_____

Activity

Life Skills: Coping

Lesson: Facing Family Problems
STRATEGIES FOR DEALING WITH PROBLEMS

Dealing with family problems can be difficult. Consider the following situation and answer the questions that follow.

Justin has moved to a new city. He is attending a new school. His parents are worried that he is having trouble adjusting. Justin refuses to talk to his parents about the move. He goes into his room and slams the door every time they try to talk with him.

1. What type of problem are Justin and his family dealing with?

_____

_____

_____

2. Write down three ways that Justin and his family could resolve this problem.

_____

_____

_____

_____

_____

3. If Justin were in danger, what three people could he talk to about the problem.

_____

_____

_____

Concept Review

Lesson: What Is Conflict?

In the blanks provided, write *I* beside the examples of internal conflict and *E* beside the examples of external conflict.

_____ **1.** Haivan and her best friend are arguing over where they are going to eat lunch.

_____ **2.** Ben is upset with himself for getting a low score on his math test.

_____ **3.** Carrie cannot decide if she should go to the movies or finish her homework.

_____ **4.** Alex is yelling at Omar for bumping him in the hallway.

_____ **5.** Judy spilled juice on a shirt she borrowed from Melissa. Melissa is angry and will not speak to Judy.

Lesson: Managing Conflict

6. List two types of communication that are important during conflict.

_____

_____

7. List three ways that a conflict can end.

_____

_____

_____

8. Why is it important to have empathy?

_____

_____

_____

9. Name a situation in which it would be best to walk away from a conflict.

_____

_____

_____

| Concept Review *continued*

In the blanks provided, write *com* beside the examples of compromise and *col* beside the examples of collaboration for each of the following conflict resolutions.

_____**10.** Pam and Lee are deciding what to do on Saturday. Pam wants to go to the zoo, but Lee wants to go to the mall. They decide to go to the zoo first, and then to the mall.

_____**11.** Jasmine and Tony are trying to pick a restaurant for dinner. Jasmine wants to eat at the Mexican restaurant and Tony wants to eat at the Italian restaurant. Since they cannot agree, they decide to eat at a Chinese restaurant instead.

_____**12.** Kyle is making chili for dinner. Kyle likes his food very spicy, but Erik likes his food milder. Kyle decides to make the chili a little spicy, but not too spicy.

_____**13.** Gina wants to paint the living room green. Martin wants to paint the living room tan. They decide to paint the room both colors.

Lesson: Anger

14. Explain what anger is.

_____

_____

_____

15. Explain the difference between anger at events and anger at others.

_____

_____

_____

_____

16. Why is it important to resolve anger at yourself?

_____

_____

_____

_____

_____

| Concept Review *continued*

Lesson: Managing Anger

17. Explain how anger can affect relationships both positively and negatively.

_____

_____

_____

18. Explain how anger can lead to violence.

_____

_____

19. List two types of signs that indicate that violence may occur.

_____

_____

Lesson: Expressing Anger

Write the letter of the correct answer in the space provided.

_____**20.** Which is NOT a healthy expression of anger?
  a. talking calmly
  b. choosing your words carefully
  c. yelling loudly
  d. keeping some distance from the other person

_____**21.** Which is a healthy expression of anger?
  a. violence
  b. aggression
  c. loud yelling
  d. calm speaking

22. What can happen if you express your anger in an unhealthy way?

_____

_____

_____

_____

| Concept Review *continued*

23. List three things you can do to help yourself stay cool when you are angry.

_____

_____

_____

Lesson: What Is Stress?

24. Define *stress*.

_____

_____

25. What problems can negative stress cause?

_____

_____

26. Describe a situation in which stress could have a positive effect.

_____

_____

Lesson: Sources of Stress

Write the letter of the correct answer in the space provided.

_____ **27.** Sources of stress can include
   a. school.
   b. friends.
   c. family.
   d. All of the above

_____ **28.** Emotions caused by stress can include
   a. fear of failing.
   b. anger toward friends.
   c. frustration.
   d. All of the above

| Concept Review *continued*

In the blanks provided, write *E* beside the examples of stress caused by events, and *O* beside the examples of stress caused by other people.

_____**29.** Yvonne is worried that she will not play well in the soccer game on Saturday.

_____**30.** Jack had an argument with his best friend at lunch today.

_____**31.** Ali is very sad because his dog died.

_____**32.** Sarah is worried that her parents will be disappointed with her grades.

Lesson: Managing Stress

33. List two ways you can prevent stressful situations.

_____

_____

_____

34. How can physical activity help you control stress?

_____

_____

_____

35. List three creative activities that can give you a break from stress.

_____

_____

_____

_____

_____

_____

Activity

Health Inventory

Lesson: Expressing Anger

Create a multimedia presentation about healthy and unhealthy ways to express anger. Your presentation should cover the following topics:

• verbal expression of anger

• body language

• violence

• staying calm

Your presentation should show at least three examples of unhealthy expressions of anger and three examples of healthy expressions of anger. Also include tips for making unhealthy expressions of anger less likely.

Lesson: What Is Stress?

Go to the library and research stress. Find at least three sources and write a three-page report on stress. Try to answer the following questions in your report:

• What are the physical symptoms of stress?

• What are the emotional effects of stress?

• What are the signs of negative stress?

• How can negative stress affect your physical and emotional health?

• How can stress affect people positively?

Your report should include an introduction, several body paragraphs, and a conclusion. When your report is complete, exchange reports with a classmate and compare your findings.

Name _____ Class _____ Date _____

Health Behavior Contract

Coping with Conflict and Stress

My Goals: I, _____, will accomplish one or more of the following goals:

I will express my anger in a healthy and constructive way.

I will practice strategies for resolving conflicts.

I will report any and all threats of violence against myself or others.

I will practice strategies for reducing stress.

Other: _____

_____

My Reasons: By expressing anger in a healthy way and using conflict management strategies, I can make sure that the conflicts I am in do not get out of control, and I can turn many of these conflicts into positive learning experiences. Also, by practicing strategies for avoiding and relieving stress, I can avoid physical problems and be happier overall.

Other: _____

_____

My Values: Personal values that will help me meet my goals are

_____

_____

_____

My Plan: The actions I will take to meet my goals are

_____

_____

_____

Evaluation: I will use my Health Journal to keep a log of actions I took to fulfill this contract. After 1 month, I will evaluate my goals. I will adjust my plan if my goals are not being met. If my goals are being met, I will consider setting additional goals.

Signed _____

Date _____

Activity

Life Skills: Communicating Effectively

Lesson: Managing Conflict
COMMUNICATING DURING CONFLICT
Read the following. Then, answer the questions.

Todd took a pencil out of Gina's backpack without asking. When Gina reached for her pencil during class, she could not find it. She noticed Todd using her pencil and got very angry. Gina confronted him after class about taking the pencil. Todd said he just needed to borrow the pencil for the day because he lost his last one. Gina became very angry and started yelling at Todd. Todd became angry too and told her he would never give the pencil back.

1. What could Todd have done differently to prevent this conflict?

_____

_____

_____

_____

2. What type of situation occurred: win-win, win-lose, or lose-lose? Explain.

_____

_____

_____

3. What could each person have done to turn this into a win-win situation?

_____

_____

_____

_____

_____

_____

_____

_____

Activity

Life Skills: Assessing Your Health

Lesson: What Is Stress?
IDENTIFYING SIGNS OF NEGATIVE STRESS
Read the following. Then, answer the questions in the space provided.

Situation A. Melanie really wants to win the school spelling bee. She finishes her homework early every night so she can spend time practicing for the spelling bee. On the weekends, she spends about five hours practicing for the spelling bee. The spelling bee is tomorrow and she feels very prepared.

Situation B. José is on the track team. There is a big meet coming up, so he has been spending more time practicing. He usually runs for a couple of hours after school each day. When he gets home, he eats dinner and then is too tired to do his homework. He has fallen behind in his classes and did poorly on his last two tests. He is really worried about his grades. Worrying so much is giving him headaches and making him very sad.

1. Which situation is an example of negative stress? _____

2. Which situation is an example of positive stress? _____

3. How is stress affecting Melanie?

_____

_____

4. How is stress affecting José?

_____

_____

5. What can José do to reduce his stress?

_____

_____

_____

6. What could happen if José does not make changes to reduce his stress?

_____

_____

_____

Skills Worksheet

Concept Review

Lesson: Caring for Your Skin

Match each term in the right column to the correct item in the left column. Write the letter in the space provided.

_____ **1.** An inflammation of the skin that happens when pores get clogged with dirt.

_____ **2.** The outer layer of the skin.

_____ **3.** They make a substance that keeps the skin soft and flexible.

_____ **4.** Bumps that form from acne.

_____ **5.** The layer of living cells below the epidermis.

a. dermis

b. acne

c. epidermis

d. pimples

e. oil glands

Fill in the blanks on the diagram with the appropriate name of the structure.

6._____ 7._____

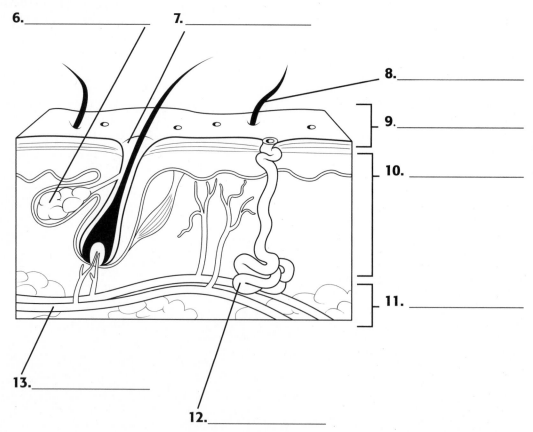

8._____

9._____

10._____

11._____

13._____

12._____

| Concept Review *continued*

Lesson: Caring for Your Hair and Nails

In the blanks provided, fill in the missing letters to spell the term being described.

14. Hair is made up of this material.   ke __ __ t __ __

15. Dried clumps of dead cells, which are flaky   __ a __ dr __ f __

16. Small insects that live on the scalp and suck blood   h __ __ d l __ __ __

17. Hair grows from here   __ o __ __ i __ l __ s

18. A thin flap of skin around the nail   c __ __ i __ le

19. List two ways to care for your hair.

_____

_____

20. List two ways to care for your nails.

_____

_____

Lesson: Caring for Your Teeth

Fill in the blanks on the diagram with the appropriate term.

21. _____

22. _____

23. _____

24. _____

25. _____

26. _____

| Concept Review *continued*

Fill in the blanks with the correct answers to complete the sentences.

_____ **27.** Plaque is a mixture of bacteria, saliva, and
        a. pulp.
        b. toothpaste.
        c. food particles.
        d. wax.

_____ **28.** Bacteria in food makes
        a. enamel.
        b. acids
        c. milk.
        d. None of the above

_____ **29.** Tooth decay can be avoided with proper
        a. medicine.
        b. rest.
        c. brushing and flossing.
        d. exercise.

_____ **30.** Teeth get minerals to keep them strong from milk and other sources of
        a. calcium.
        b. dentin.
        c. pulp.
        d. None of the above

Lesson: Caring for Your Eyes

Match each definition with the correct term. Write the letter in the space provided.

_____ **31.** the clear, protective structure at the front of the eye

_____ **32.** the colorful part of the eye

_____ **33.** the part of the eye that contains millions of light-sensitive cells

_____ **34.** the hole in the iris

_____ **35.** part of the eye that focuses the light on the retina

a. cornea

b. iris

c. retina

d. pupil

e. lens

| Concept Review *continued*

36. Describe a common eye problem and how it can be treated.

_____

_____

_____

_____

_____

Lesson: Caring for Your Ears
Label the diagram of the ear by writing the name of each part on the correct line.

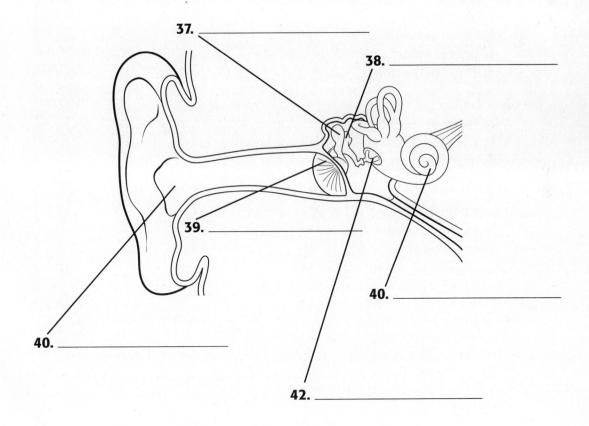

37. _____

38. _____

39. _____

40. _____

40. _____

42. _____

| Concept Review *continued*

43. List three common hearing problems.

_____

_____

_____

Lesson: Healthcare Resources

Write the letter of the correct answer in the space provided.

_____**44.** A healthcare consumer is one who buys
  a. healthcare products only.
  b. healthcare services only.
  c. Both A and B
  d. None of the above

_____**45.** Healthcare purchases can be influenced by advertising, tradition, and
  a. air pressure.
  b. blood pressure.
  c. peer pressure.
  d. None of the above

_____**46.** A healthcare provider is any professional who
  a. helps people stay healthy.
  b. pays for healthcare products or services.
  c. works for the government.
  d. None of the above.

_____**47.** Local healthcare agencies protect your health by
  a. making sure the drinking water is clean.
  b. collecting trash and garbage.
  c. inspecting restaurant kitchens.
  d. All of the above

_____**48.** The federal government and other national organizations also play a role in healthcare by
  a. conducting research to help develop treatments for disease.
  b. sending us cards when we are not feeling well.
  c. approving both foods and drugs for widespread use.
  d. Both A and C

Concept Review *continued*

Give the definition of each of the following terms.

49. healthcare consumer

_____

_____

50. unit price

_____

_____

51. healthcare provider

_____

_____

52. orthodontist

_____

_____

53. general practitioner

_____

_____

54. specialist

_____

_____

Name _____ Class _____ Date _____

Caring For Your Body

Read each statement below. Decide whether it describes how you take responsibility for your body. Write *always, sometimes,* **or** *never* **in the space to the left of each statement.**

_____ **1.** I am aware of my personal care habits, both positive and negative.

_____ **2.** I bathe regularly and take care of my skin.

_____ **3.** I take care of my hair and my nails by keeping them clean.

_____ **4.** I brush and floss my teeth.

_____ **5.** I see the dentist at least twice a year to check my teeth and gums.

_____ **6.** I eat a healthy diet to make sure my teeth and gums will remain healthy.

_____ **7.** I gather as much information as possible before buying a healthcare product.

_____ **8.** I protect my eyes in the sun, when I'm working with tools, and when I am playing sports.

_____ **9.** I keep my ears healthy and working well by protecting them from loud sounds.

_____ **10.** I communicate with my healthcare provider when I see him or her for my annual physical exams.

Score yourself: Give yourself 3 points for each *always* **answer, 1 point for each** *sometimes,* **and 0 for each** *never.* **Write your score here _____.**

30–25: Excellent—You always take responsibility for your body.

24–20: Good—You often take responsibility for your body.

19–15: Fair—You are taking some responsibility for your body, but you can improve.

Fewer than 15: You need to work on taking responsibility for your body

Name _____ Class _____ Date _____

Health Behavior Contract

Caring for Your Body

My Goals: I, _____, will accomplish one or
more of the following goals:

I will take care of my skin.

I will take care of my teeth.

I will shop for healthcare products carefully.

Other: _____

_____

My Reasons: By taking care of my body and shopping carefully for healthcare
products, I can live a healthier life.

Other: _____

_____

My Values: Personal values that will help me meet my goals are

_____

_____

_____

My Plan: The actions I will take to meet my goals are

_____

_____

_____

Evaluation: I will use my Health Journal to keep a log of actions I took to fulfill
this contract. After 1 month, I will evaluate my goals. I will adjust my plan if my
goals are not being met. If my goals are being met, I will consider setting additional goals.

Signed _____

Date _____

Name _____ Class _____ Date _____

Life Skills: Assessing Your Health

Lesson: Caring for Your Teeth
EVALUATING YOUR DIET

It is easy not to eat properly when you are in your pre-teen and teen years. Not eating properly and changes in your diet affect your teeth. Besides proper brushing and flossing, watching your diet has a lot to do with the health of both your teeth and your gums. Keeping track of what you eat by keeping a food journal can help you to stay on track by eating the proper amounts of fruits, vegetables, and sources of calcium.

Follow these guidelines to help you to stay on track with a healthy diet!

1. **Eat 5 servings of fruits and vegetables a day.** Some green vegetables have the mineral calcium, which helps to build strong teeth. Eating fruits and vegetables keeps your heart healthy, too.

2. **Eat 3 servings of milk and dairy products a day** Not only do milk dairy milk products provide the calcium you need for better gums and stronger teeth, they also provide you with protein and zinc. Zinc helps to build your immune system which fights off infections. Infections in the mouth can cause damage to your mouth and gums.

3. **Eat 6 to 11 servings from the bread, cereal, rice, and pasta group.** Whole grains provide fiber and other nutrients. This helps to build a strong body and to get rid of wastes in your body as well.

4. **Remember to limit your intake of fried foods.** Baking or broiling meat and eating fresh fruits and vegetables helps provide the nutrients you need to build strong teeth and keep your gums healthy.

Start a food journal today. Write down all the foods you eat at the end of the day, compare how you did in terms of the four guidelines. Note where you can make improvements.

Activity

Life Skills: Evaluating Media Messages

Lesson: Healthcare Resources
ANALYZING MAGAZINE ADS FOR INFORMATION OF NAME BRANDS

Look through several magazine ads that advertise healthcare products. Compare the difference in the way each ad presents a product. What in the ad might make a consumer want to purchase one type of personal product over another? Answer the following questions.

1. Select a hair product and identify the audience that is being targeted for the product you have picked. What is effective about the advertisement?

_____

_____

2. Identify a product for skincare that is being advertised. Does the advertiser make any false claims in its advertisement? How could you find out?

_____

_____

_____

3. Are personal products being advertised that a smart consumer does NOT need to use? How could you tell?

_____

_____

_____

4. Pick two ads for competing healthcare products. Compare the way one is advertised over the other. What are some product benefits mentioned in the ad? Might a consumer see any drawbacks to using the products, based on the ads?

_____

_____

_____

_____

_____

_____

Skills Worksheet

Concept Review

Lesson: Body Systems

Fill in each blank in the first column with the name of the body system described in the second column.

BODY SYSTEM	FUNCTIONS
_____	**1.** transports nutrients, oxygen, and hormones throughout the body; transports waste products
_____	**2.** supports the body; stores minerals such as calcium and phosphorus
_____	**3.** exchanges air between the environment and the lungs; filters materials from the air before it enters the lungs
_____	**4.** enables the body to respond to changes in the environment; controls the activities of the organs and the body systems

In the blanks provided, fill in the letter of the term or phrase being described.

5. a group of similar cells working together __ __ s s __ __

6. the basic unit of all living things __ e __ __

7. a group of tissues that work together __ r __ __ n

8. a group of organs that work together __ o __ __   __ y __ __ e__

9. How can a problem in one body system affect another body system?

_____

_____

Lesson: The Skeletal System

Match the definitions with the correct term. Write the letter in the space provided.

_____**10.** a place where two or more bones meet

_____**11.** an organ of the skeletal system

_____**12.** soft tissue inside a bone

a. bone marrow
b. joint
c. bone

| **Concept Review** *continued* |

13. List two functions of the skeletal system.

_____

_____

14. What is one possible change in the skeletal system associated with age?

_____

Lesson: The Muscular System

15. The type of muscle that is attached to bone is _____ muscle.

16. The type of muscle that forms the heart is _____ muscle.

17. The type of muscle that forms some internal organs is

_____ muscle.

Examine the diagram below, and answer the questions that follow.

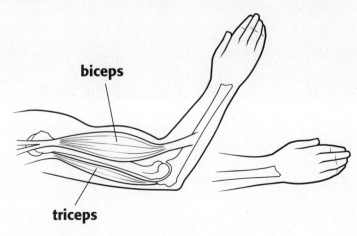

18. Which of the muscles shown in the diagram above contracts to bend the elbow?

_____

19. Which of the muscles shown in the diagram above contracts to straighten the elbow?

_____

| Concept Review *continued*

Lesson: The Digestive System

Fill in the blanks below to describe what parts of the digestive process occur in each part of the digestive system.

20. mouth

_____

_____

21. pharynx and esophagus

_____

_____

22. stomach

_____

_____

23. small intestine

_____

_____

24. large intestine

_____

_____

25. Define the following terms:

   a. nutrients

_____

_____

   b. digestion

_____

_____

26. List four ways that your body gets rid of waste products.

_____

_____

_____

_____

Name _____ Class _____ Date _____

| Concept Review *continued*

Lesson: The Circulatory System

27. List two functions of the circulatory system.

_____

_____

28. Define the following terms:

a. artery

_____

_____

b. vein

_____

_____

c. capillary

_____

_____

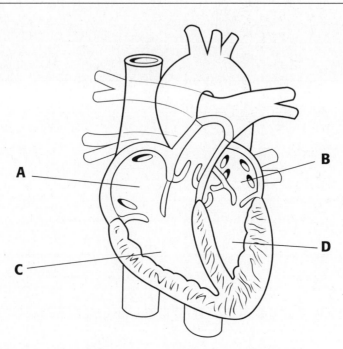

Write the name of each labeled part on the correct line below.

29. A. _____   **C.** _____

     B. _____   **D.** _____

| Concept Review *continued*

Fill in the blanks to describe the flow of blood in the heart.

The **30.** _____ pumps blood to the lungs. Gas exchange takes

place in the lungs, and then the blood flows to the **31.** _____.

The blood is then pumped into the **32.** _____, which pumps

blood to the body. From the body, the blood flows to the

33. _____ of the heart.

Lesson: The Respiratory System

34. Define the following terms:

   a. diaphragm

_____

_____

   b. trachea

_____

_____

   c. lung

_____

_____

   d. inhalation

_____

_____

   e. exhalation

_____

_____

35. The important gas that enters the blood in the alveoli is called

_____.

36. The waste gas that is removed from the blood in the alveoli is called

_____.

| Concept Review *continued*

Lesson: The Nervous System

In the blanks provided, fill in the letters of the term being described.

37. an organ that carries messages to and from the brain

 __ __ i n __ __   __ o __ __

38. a bundle of cells that conducts messages from one part of the body to another

 __ e __ __ e

39. an automatic response to a stimulus   __ e __ __ e __

40. the major organ of the nervous system   __ r __ __ n

41. List two functions of the nervous system.

 _____

 _____

Lesson: Taking Care of Your Body Systems

42. Explain how exercise benefits your heart and the muscles of the respiratory system.

 _____

43. How can healthy foods help your body to function properly?

 _____

44. Unlike illegal drugs, alcohol is legally sold to adults. Why should people still be very careful about drinking alcoholic beverages?

 _____

 _____

45. Why is refusing drugs an important way to care for your body?

 _____

46. How can sleep help your body to function properly?

 _____

47. Why is drinking enough water important for good health?

 _____

Name _____ Class _____ Date _____

Health Inventory

Your Body Systems

Read each statement below. Write *always, sometimes,* or *never* in the space to the left of each statement.

_____ **1.** I get plenty of exercise.

_____ **2.** I eat a variety of healthy foods.

_____ **3.** I avoid all tobacco products.

_____ **4.** I don't drink alcoholic beverages.

_____ **5.** I refuse illegal drugs.

_____ **6.** I get plenty of sleep.

_____ **7.** I drink plenty of water.

_____ **8.** I chew my food thoroughly.

_____ **9.** I eat food high in calcium.

_____ **10.** I maintain good posture. I do not slouch when I sit or stand.

_____ **11.** I eat fruits and vegetables every day.

_____ **12.** I eat grains like bread and cereals to get energy.

Score yourself. Give yourself 2 points for each *always* answer, 1 point for each *sometimes* answer, and 0 points for each *never* answer. Write your score here:

_____

19 to 24 points: Excellent: You have learned how to keep your body systems healthy.

11 to 18 points: Good: You often make choices that will keep your body systems healthy.

0 to 10 points: You need to learn more about keeping your body systems healthy.

Name _____ Class _____ Date _____

> **Activity**

Health Behavior Contract

Your Body System

My Goals: I, _____, will accomplish one or more of the following goals:

I will exercise regularly.

I will drink enough water and eat a balanced diet.

I will use refusal skills if someone offers me tobacco products or other drugs.

Other: _____

_____

My Reasons: By practicing health habits that improve the health of my body systems, I will help keep my body healthy now and for the rest of my life. By avoiding tobacco and other drugs, I will protect my body systems from harm.

Other: _____

_____

My Values: Personal values that will help me meet my goals are

_____

_____

_____

My Plan: The actions I will take to meet my goals are

_____

_____

_____

_____

Evaluation: I will use my Health Journal to keep a log of actions I took to fulfill this contract. After 1 month, I will evaluate my goals. I will adjust my plan if my goals are not being met. If my goals are being met, I will consider setting additional goals.

Signed _____

Date _____

Name _____ Class _____ Date _____

Life Skills: Assessing Your Health

Lesson: The Skeletal System
HEALTHY BONES

Calcium is one of the minerals required to build and maintain healthy bones. Adequate calcium intake throughout a lifetime can help reduce the risk of osteoporosis. The recommended daily intake of calcium for 9- to 13-year-olds is 1,300 mg. Use the table below to record the amount of calcium you consume in one day. The amount of calcium in foods can be found on food labels. Sometimes you don't have access to food labels. You can use reliable Internet sites and other research materials to find the amount of calcium in foods if the label in not available. After you have completed the table, review your results and brainstorm ways to include more calcium in your diet.

Food/Amount Consumed	Amount of Calcium
Total Calcium	

Name _____ Class _____ Date _____

Life Skills: Setting Goals

Lesson: The Circulatory System
EXERCISE GOALS

The health of your circulatory system affects the health of every other system in your body. One way to improve and maintain the health of your circulatory system is to take part in physical activity. Exercise and other physical activity strengthens your heart, increasing the efficiency at which it pumps blood through your body. In this activity, you will examine ways that you can incorporate physical activity into your life, and set goals for the amount of physical activity you will perform.

1. List the physical activities, exercises, or sports in which you are active.

_____

_____

_____

_____

2. How often do you participate in physical education at school?

_____

_____

_____

3. List some other ways you get exercise while going about your daily activities, for example, walking to school.

_____

_____

_____

_____

_____

_____

| Life Skills *continued*

4. Examine your answers to questions 1, 2, and 3. Consider the types of activities in which you are interested. Use the information to set three goals for increasing or maintaining your level of physical activity. Each goal should list a specific activity, the frequency of the activity, and a time frame for meeting the goal.

a. _____

_____

_____

_____

_____

_____

b. _____

_____

_____

_____

_____

_____

c. _____

_____

_____

_____

_____

_____

_____

Skills Worksheet

Concept Review

Lesson: Human Reproduction

_____ 1. The sex cells made by males are called
   a. testes.
   b. eggs.
   c. sperm.
   d. ovaries.

_____ 2. The sex cells made by females are called
   a. testes.
   b. eggs.
   c. sperm.
   d. ovaries.

3. The _____ make sperm and testosterone.

4. The _____ are the organs that make eggs and the

hormones estrogen and progesterone.

5. The monthly breakdown and shedding of the lining of the uterus is called

_____ .

6. List five ways to protect your reproductive health.

_____

_____

_____

_____

Lesson: Before You Were Born

7. Describe the process of fertilization.

_____

_____

_____

8. The developing human inside the uterus is called a _____ .

| **Concept Review** *continued*

9. At what point during the development of a fetus are the organs fully functional?

_____

_____

10. Describe three factors that affect the health of both the mother and fetus.

_____

_____

_____

Lesson: Infancy and Childhood

_____**11.** The time between birth and 1 year of age is called
  a. infancy.
  b. childhood.
  c. adolescence.
  d. adulthood.

12. List the three stages of childhood development.

_____

_____

_____

13. What are the characteristics of middle childhood?

_____

_____

_____

Lesson: Adolescence

Match each word in the right column with the definition in the left column. Write the letter in the space provided.

_____**14.** a chemical made in one part of the body that causes a change in a different part of the body

_____**15.** the stage of development when the reproductive system becomes mature

_____**16.** the stage of development in which humans grow from childhood to adulthood

a. adolescence

b. hormone

c. puberty

▌Concept Review *continued*

17. What effects do sex hormones have on the body?

_____

_____

_____

_____

18. Describe three physical changes that happen to boys during adolescence.

_____

_____

_____

_____

19. Describe three physical changes that happen to girls during adolescence.

_____

_____

_____

_____

20. List four mental and emotional changes that occur during adolescence.

_____

_____

_____

_____

Lesson: Adulthood, Aging, and Death

21. Describe adulthood.

_____

_____

_____

_____

| Concept Review *continued*

22. Explain how technology has affected life expectancy in the United States.

_____

_____

_____

_____

_____

_____

23. List the stages of grief.

_____

_____

_____

_____

_____

Activity

Health Inventory

Growth and Development

Read each of the following statements. Think about how well it describes your behavior. Then write *always*, *sometimes*, or *never* in the space next to each statement.

_____ **1.** I go along with whatever my friends are doing.

_____ **2.** I will do something to fit in, even though I know it is dangerous.

_____ **3.** If a friend offers me alcohol, I will accept it just to fit in.

_____ **4.** If someone tells me smoking is cool, I will try smoking.

_____ **5.** It is difficult for me to say no.

_____ **6.** If a friend were to offer me drugs, I would accept them just to fit in.

_____ **7.** It is difficult for me to walk away from unhealthy situations.

_____ **8.** I'm afraid someone will make fun of me if I don't do the things my friends do, even if they are unhealthy.

_____ **9.** I find myself doing things I don't want to do just because everyone else is doing them.

Score yourself on this quiz. Give yourself 0 points for each *always*, 3 points for each *sometimes*, and 5 points for each *never*. Write your score here _____.

Less than 25: Excellent—You are on top of your health and in control of your life.

25–29: Good—You recognize the need to care for yourself and often do so.

35–39: Fair—You are working on some areas of health, but you need to focus on improving your overall life skills.

40–45: You need to focus on your health and wellness. Examine the nine life skills and choose a starting point.

Name _____ Class _____ Date _____

Activity

Health Behavior Contract

Growth and Development

My Goals: I, _____, will accomplish one or more of the following goals:

I will be more informed about my reproductive health.

I will talk with my parent or guardian about reproductive health.

I will perform monthly physical self-examinations and schedule regular medical checkups.

Other: _____

_____

My Reasons: By improving my awareness of my reproductive health, I will be able to make good choices, such as abstaining from sexual activity. I will be able to take better care of my body by performing self-examinations and having regular medical checkups.

Other: _____

_____

My Values: Personal values that will help me meet my goals are

_____

_____

My Plan: The actions I will take to meet my goals are

_____

_____

Evaluation: I will use my Health Journal to keep a log of actions I took to fulfill this contract. After 1 month, I will evaluate my goals. I will adjust my plan if my goals are not being met. If my goals are being met, I will consider setting additional goals.

Signed _____

Date _____

Name _____ Class _____ Date _____

Life Skills: Evaluating Media Messages

Lesson: Adolescence
ADVERTISING FOR ADOLESCENTS

Watch TV commercials and look at magazine advertisements. Pick out advertisements that target adolescents. Identify the types of products that are marketed to adolescents and the techniques advertisers use to reach the adolescent audience.

1. What types of products are advertised to adolescents?

_____

_____

_____

2. Are more advertisements targeted at boys or at girls? Explain your answer.

_____

_____

_____

3. What techniques do advertisers use to get the attention of adolescents?

_____

_____

_____

4. Which advertising techniques do you think are most effective? Why?

_____

_____

_____

5. Pick the most effective advertisement you found and describe it below. What makes it so effective?

_____

_____

_____

_____

Activity

Life Skills: Coping

Lesson: Adulthood, Aging, and Death
COPING WITH GRIEF

Your friend Kelly lives far away from you. Her grandmother just passed away. Imagine that you received the letter below from Kelly. Write a letter in return that gives Kelly suggestions for coping with her grief.

Dear Friend,

How are you? I'm not doing very well right now. Grandma just died last week. I still can't believe that she's gone. It just doesn't feel real. The funeral was yesterday and it was so sad. I don't know what I'll do without Grandma. I loved her so much.

I hope everything is OK with you.

Your friend,

Kelly

_____

_____

_____

_____

_____

_____

_____

_____

_____

_____

_____

_____

_____

_____

Skills Worksheet

Concept Review

Lesson: Disease and Your Body

Match definition with the correct term. Write the letter in space provided.

_____ **1.** anything that causes disease

_____ **2.** any harmful change in your state of health

_____ **3.** a disease that is not caused by a virus or living organism

_____ **4.** tissues, organs, and cells that fight disease

_____ **5.** a disease caused by a pathogen

a. immune system
b. disease
c. noninfectious disease
d. infectious disease
e. pathogen

6. What is one way that infectious diseases and noninfectious diseases are alike?

_____

_____

7. What is one way that infectious diseases and noninfectious diseases are different?

_____

_____

8. Explain how your immune system fights disease.

_____

_____

Lesson: Infectious Diseases

In the blanks provided, define the following terms.

9. virus

_____

_____

10. bacteria

_____

_____

11. protists

_____

_____

12. fungi

_____

_____

13. List four causes of infectious diseases.

_____

_____

_____

_____

14. Name and describe two strategies to reduce the spread of common infectious diseases in your home.

_____

_____

Lesson: Controlling Infectious Diseases

15. What are two strategies you can use to protect yourself from infectious diseases?

_____

_____

16. List two strategies for protecting others from infectious diseases.

_____

_____

17. If you get a vaccine, how does it protect others from infectious diseases?

_____

_____

Lesson: Sexually Transmitted Diseases

18. Name five common sexually transmitted diseases, and list one symptom of each.

_____

_____

_____

_____

_____

19. What is the one way to be absolutely sure you will not get an STD?

_____

_____

20. Explain how HIV weakens the immune system.

_____

_____

21. Can all STDs be cured? Explain your answer.

_____

_____

In the blank provided, define the following terms.

22. sexually transmitted disease

_____

_____

23. AIDS

_____

_____

24. abstinence

_____

_____

Lesson: Noninfectious Diseases

In the blanks provided, fill in the letters of the term or phrase being described.

25. disease or disorder not caused by a virus or living organism is called

_ _ _ I _ F _ _ T _ _ U _

26. a disease present at birth that is not a genetic disease is called

_ O _ G _ N _ _ A _

27. a disease caused by information passed from one or both parents is called

_ E _ E _ _ C

28. List three common noninfectious diseases.

_____

_____

_____

29. What is the difference between a congenital disease and a genetic disease?

_____

_____

_____

30. What is one noninfectious disease related to a lifestyle choice?

_____

_____

31. What is one noninfectious disease related to a person's surroundings?

_____

_____

_____

Activity

Health Inventory

Controlling Disease

Read each statement below. Think about how well it describes your behavior. Write *always, sometimes,* **or** *never* **in the space to the left of each statement.**

_____ **1.** I eat a healthy diet.

_____ **2.** I exercise every day.

_____ **3.** I avoid all tobacco products.

_____ **4.** I wash my hands before I eat.

_____ **5.** I wash my hands after I use the restroom.

_____ **6.** I avoid alcoholic beverages.

_____ **7.** I get plenty of rest.

_____ **8.** I cope with the stress in my life.

_____ **9.** I stay away from people who have an infectious disease.

_____ **10.** I receive my vaccines on schedule.

Score yourself. Give yourself 2 points for each *always* **answer, 1 point for each** *sometimes* **answer, and 0 points for each** *never* **answer. Write your score here.**

_____

25–30: Excellent: You have learned how to reduce your risk of disease.
20–25: Good: You have made some choices that will help you avoid disease.
10–20: Fair: You can improve your choices and reduce your risk of disease.
0–10: You should work on your choices to reduce your risk factors for disease.

Name _____ Class _____ Date _____

Health Behavior Contract

Controlling Disease

My Goals: I, _____, will accomplish one or more of the following goals:

I will take steps to lower my risk of catching infectious diseases.

I will practice good hygiene.

I will exercise regularly, eat a healthy diet, and get plenty of sleep.

I will ask my family if I am at risk for any hereditary or other noninfectious diseases.

Other: _____

_____

My Reasons: By practicing good hygiene, I will avoid catching and spreading many diseases. By exercising regularly, eating a healthy diet, and getting enough sleep, I will help protect my body from disease. By asking my family about my risks for diseases, I will be able to watch for warning signs of the disease and I will be able to modify my lifestyle to reduce the risks.

Other: _____

_____

My Values: Personal values that will help me meet my goals are

_____

_____

_____

My Plan: The actions I will take to meet my goals are

_____

_____

_____

Evaluation: I will use my Health Journal to keep a log of actions I took to fulfill this contract. After 1 month, I will evaluate my goals. I will adjust my plan if my goals are not being met. If my goals are being met, I will consider setting additional goals.

Signed _____

Date _____

Activity

Life Skills: Practicing Wellness

Lesson: Controlling Infectious Diseases
HAND WASHING ANALYSIS

There are many ways to stop or slow the spread of infectious diseases. According to the Centers for Disease Control and Prevention, one of the most effective methods to protect yourself and other from infectious disease is to practice proper hand washing. The following are times when you should wash your hands: Before, during, and after food preparation or handling, before you eat, after you use the restroom, after handling animals, and when your hands appear dirty.

The proper method for hand washing is: wet your hands with warm water, use soap and scrub for about 15 seconds, rinse with warm water, and then thoroughly dry your hands.

Use the following table to record the number of times you wash your hands in one day, and whether or not you use the proper washing technique. After you have completed the chart, evaluate your hand washing habits.

Time of Day	Reason for Hand Washing	Proper Technique?

1. Were there times during the day when you should have washed your hands, but weren't able to?

_____

_____

2. How could you improve your hand-washing habits?

_____

_____

Name _____ Class _____ Date _____

Life Skills: Communicating Effectively

Lesson: Noninfectious Diseases
COMMUNICATION SKILLS

There are many noninfectious diseases that affect people of your age. These diseases are not contagious and can't be passed from person to person. Some noninfectious diseases limit or restrict foods people can eat, the activities they can take part in, or their ability to learn. However, noninfectious diseases do not stop people from being happy, productive students and good friends. Tell how you would use effective communication skills in the following situations.

1. A student in your class needs more time to learn concepts than many of the other students. You know that this student has a noninfectious disease that affects the speed at which he can learn. One day you hear some of your friends making fun of this student. What would your response be?

_____

_____

_____

_____

2. Your classmate Jose has diabetes. He needs to monitor his blood glucose levels throughout the day. Some younger students try to avoid sitting by Jose at lunch—they say they don't want to catch his diabetes. What would you say to these students?

_____

_____

_____

_____

3. Emily's asthma occasionally acts up during school. The other day she needed to use her inhaler several times. Some of the other girls in class said she was just trying to find a way to avoid gym class. How could you tell them that Emily's asthma usually doesn't limit her activities?

_____

_____

_____

_____

Name _____ Class _____ Date _____

Concept Review

Lesson: What Is Physical Fitness?

1. Define *physical fitness*.

_____

_____

FOUR PARTS OF PHYSICAL FITNESS

2. List the four parts of physical fitness.

_____

_____

_____

_____

PHYSICAL BENEFITS OF EXERCISE

3. Describe five physical improvements in the body from exercise.

_____

_____

_____

OTHER BENEFITS OF EXERCISE

4. Describe one mental benefit of exercise.

_____

_____

5. Describe one emotional benefit of exercise.

_____

_____

6. Describe one social benefit of exercise.

_____

_____

Lesson: Your Fitness and Goals

VISITING THE DOCTOR

7. List two things a doctor might want to know from your health history.

_____

_____

_____

8. A _____ is a medical checkup to make sure you can play the sport safely.

TESTING YOUR FITNESS

9. What are the healthy fitness zones for a 13-year-old boy?

_____

_____

_____

_____

CHOOSING YOUR ACTIVITIES

10. Use your _____ to choose physical activities.

11. A _____ is a goal to improve your physical fitness.

INFLUENCES ON YOUR GOALS

12. Set _____ goals to help you meet long-term goals.

13. List two things that can affect your fitness goals.

_____

_____

_____

| Concept Review *continued*

Lesson: Meeting Your Goals
FREQUENCY, INTENSITY, AND TIME

14. List and describe the three things you can change to meet personal fitness goals.

_____

_____

_____

_____

_____

_____

CHECKING YOUR HEART RATE

15. Your resting heart rate _____ as your physical fitness improves.

16. Your recovery time _____ as your physical fitness improves.

17. To improve your endurance, you need to exercise in a range of higher heart rates called the _____ .

Lesson: Sports
TYPES OF SPORTS

18. _____ is a contest between two or more individuals or teams.

19. List three individual sports and three team sports.

_____

_____

_____

_____

_____

| Concept Review *continued*

BENEFITS OF SPORTS

20. Describe six benefits of sports.

_____

_____

_____

_____

_____

_____

Lesson: Injury
WARNING SIGNS OF INJURY

21. _____ is caused by hard exercise, but it is not a sign of

injury.

22. Identify the three warning signs of injuries.

_____

_____

_____

FIRST AID FOR INJURY

23. RICE can help the body heal. Identify and describe the RICE steps.

_____

_____

_____

_____

STRAINS

24. A strain is an injury in which _____ or

_____ have been stretched too far or torn.

| Concept Review *continued*

SPRAINS

25. A sprain is an injury in which the _____ in the joint are stretched too far or torn.

FRACTURES

26. A fracture is a cracked or broken _____ .

Lesson: Avoiding Injury While Exercising

27. Most injuries can be avoided by _____ .

WARMING UP

28. A _____ is any activity you do to get your body ready for exercise.

29. A warm-up loosens _____ , increases

_____ , and slightly raises _____ .

COOLING DOWN

30. A _____ is any activity that helps your body return to the way it was before exercising.

31. What are two activities you could use for a good cool-down?

_____

_____

STRETCHING

32. What are two benefits of stretching?

_____

_____

33. What movement can cause an injury while stretching?

_____

34. Name two stretches you can do for leg muscles.

_____

_____

Concept Review *continued*

LESSON: SAFETY EQUIPMENT

35. Many physical activities are unsafe if you don't use _____.

WHY USE SAFETY EQUIPMENT?

36. Safety equipment protects you from _____ and makes

sports more _____.

EXAMPLES OF SAFETY EQUIPMENT

37. List examples of safety equipment for six sports.

_____

_____

_____

_____

_____

_____

Name _____ Class _____ Date _____

Activity

Health Inventory

Physical Fitness

Use the following questions to help you evaluate your physical fitness behavior. Give yourself the points at the right if you answer "yes."

yes no

❏ ❏   **1.** Are you now doing endurance exercise   20 points
             at least three times each week?

❏ ❏   **2.** Are you now doing exercise that requires strength   15 points
             at least three times each week?

❏ ❏   **3.** Do you regularly warm-up and cool-down?   10 points

❏ ❏   **4.** Do you ALWAYS use the right safety equipment?   5 points

❏ ❏   **5.** Do you regularly have a medical checkup?   5 points

❏ ❏   **6.** Do people around you think that fitness is important?   5 points

❏ ❏   **7.** Are you in the healthy fitness zone for pull-ups?   10 points

❏ ❏   **8.** Are you in the healthy fitness zone for curl-ups?   10 points

❏ ❏   **9.** Are you in the healthy fitness zone for the 1-mile run?   10 points

❏ ❏   **10.** Are you in the healthy fitness zone for the sit & reach? 10 points

Add up the points for all of the questions to which you answered "yes." _____

Circle on the scale below how your fitness behavior rates.

SCALE	
85 to 100 points	Wow! You are physically fit and are working to stay there!
65 to 80 points	Good job! Most of the time you are behaving physically fit. Think about your choices more often.
50 to 60 points	Pretty good! More than half of the time you are doing things that keep you fit. There are a few parts, however, that need work.
30 to 45 points	Pick it up! You are doing some things that aid physical fitness but there are many more things you could do.
Under 30 points	Get going! Doing more for your physical fitness will help you stay healthy.

Name _____ Class _____ Date _____

Health Behavior Contract

Physical Fitness

My Goals: I, _____, will accomplish one or more of the following goals:

I will exercise at least three times a week.

I will join a sports team.

I will improve my physical fitness by adjusting the frequency, intensity, and time of my exercise.

Other: _____

_____

My Reasons: By exercising, I will improve my physical fitness. My mental, emotional, and social health will also benefit. If I improve my physical fitness, I can avoid diseases such as heart disease, diabetes, and obesity.

Other: _____

_____

My Values: Personal values that will help me meet my goals are

_____

_____

_____

My Plan: The actions I will take to meet my goals are

_____

_____

_____

Evaluation: I will use my Health Journal to keep a log of actions I took to fulfill this contract. After 1 month, I will evaluate my goals. I will adjust my plan if my goals are not being met. If my goals are being met, I will consider setting additional goals.

Signed _____

Date _____

Name _____ Class _____ Date _____

Life Skills: Setting Goals

Lesson: Your Fitness and Goals
FITNESS GOAL ACTION PLAN

Read the following steps for setting and meeting a goal. Then, write down your responses in the spaces provided.

1. Write down your fitness goal. Think of a part of physical fitness you most want to change. Is it strength, endurance, flexibility, or body composition?

I want to change this part of physical fitness: _____

2. Make a list of the steps you will follow to reach your goal. Write down when you will start working on the change and what activities you will do. Map out the days of the week for your workouts. Will you be exercising every day or every other day? Will training on the weekend days be different? Also, identify the specific drills or exercises you will do. What will the warm-up and cool-down activities be?

I want to start my training on this date: _____

I will make the change using this activity: _____

I will exercise on these days: _____

The following are my warm-up exercises: _____

The following are my training exercises: _____

3. Do some research. See if you need more information on how to do the activities or what equipment you may need to measure progress.

4. Estimate how long it will take to reach the goal. When will the change be completed?

I want to meet my goal by this date: _____

5. Check your progress. How will you measure your progress? Where will you record the results?

I will measure my progress toward my goal by: _____

_____

6. Reward yourself. Write down what reward you will give yourself for meeting the goal. Is it something you like to do? Is it something you will purchase?

When I meet my goal I will reward myself by: _____

Name _____ Class _____ Date _____

Activity

Life Skills: Practicing Wellness

Lesson: Avoiding Injury While Exercising
PLANNING TO AVOID INJURY

Read the following steps for avoiding injury while exercising. Then, write down your responses in the spaces provided.

Warming Up. A fast walk or slow jog increases heart rate, blood flow, and body temperature. This helps muscles work and reduces the chance of muscle injury. Other arm or leg movements can also prepare muscles for action. What warm-up activities are good choices for the exercise you do?

Stretching. After the muscles are warm, stretching exercises will make them more able to move freely. The stretching exercises can involve a large part of the body or small areas of the body. What stretches should you do?

Cooling Down. Just as important as warming up to get the body going, cooling down helps the muscles relax. Stretching after a fast walk or slow jog will safely conclude the exercise session. Which activity and stretches will cool you down?

1. I plan to do these warm-up activities: _____

_____

_____

_____

2. These are some of the stretches I will do: _____

_____

_____

_____

_____

3. My cool-down activities will be: _____

_____

_____

_____

_____

Name _____ Class _____ Date _____

Concept Review

Lesson: Nutrition and Your Health

1. In the blanks provided below, using the numbers *1* through *5*, list the order in which food passes through the body.

_____ esophagus

_____ blood

_____ intestines

_____ mouth

_____ stomach

2. What is the difference between eating and nutrition?

_____

_____

_____

3. You will get hungry if you don't eat. List some other things that may happen to your body if you don't eat.

_____

_____

_____

_____

4. Is nutrition one of the most important parts of good health? Explain your answer.

_____

_____

_____

| Concept Review *continued*

Lesson: The Nutrients You Need

Complete the crossword below.

5.

Across

2. A kind of mineral that helps build strong bones

6. Helps to build strong muscles

7. These nutrients provide a LOT of energy

8. The number of classes of essential nutrients

Down

1. The most important nutrient

3. Chemicals made up of sugars chained together

4. An element from nature that helps you stay healthy

5. Help your body function and fight germs

Match the definitions with the correct term. Write the letter in the space provided.

_____ **6.** carbohydrates

_____ **7.** fats

_____ **8.** water

_____ **9.** protein

_____ **10.** vitamins

_____ **11.** minerals

a. store energy
b. fight germs
c. are sugars or starches
d. help the body function
e. prevents dehydration
f. builds muscles

Lesson: Eating for Life

Review the MyPyramid symbol below. Match each food group or type in the left column with an example of a food item from that group in the right column. Write the letter in the space provided.

_____**12.** oils

_____**13.** meat and beans

_____**14.** milk

_____**15.** vegetables

_____**16.** fruits

_____**17.** grains

a. raisins

b. broccoli

c. canola oil

d. pecans

e. oatmeal

f. yogurt

Complete each item below.

18. The _____ symbol shows you the relative proportion of your daily diet that should be made up of foods from each group.

19. The _____ label shows you how many nutrients and Calories are in a food.

20. The widest stripe on the MyPyramid symbol represents the

_____ group.

21. The thinnest stripe on the MyPyramid symbol represents

_____ .

22. The blue stripe on the MyPyramid symbol represents the

_____ group.

23. The purple stripe on the MyPyramid symbol represents the

_____ group.

24. The person climbing the steps of the MyPyramid symbol represents the

importance of _____ to a person's health.

25. The _____ for Americans can help you make healthy food choices.

Name _____ Class _____ Date _____

Health Inventory

Nutrition

Read each statement below. Decide whether it describes how you take responsibility for your decisions. Write *always, sometimes,* or *never* in the space to the left of each statement.

_____ **1.** I am aware of my eating habits, both positive and negative.

_____ **2.** I know that some of my favorite foods may not be the most healthy, and I limit how much of them I eat.

_____ **3.** I base my food choices on what I know about nutrients, not just how good a food tastes.

_____ **4.** I understand that the food choices I make could affect my health.

_____ **5.** When choosing what to eat, I keep in mind what I've already eaten that day.

_____ **6.** I remember the recommendations of the MyPyramid food guidance system when I choose what food to eat.

_____ **7.** I make the six classes of essential nutrients part of a balanced diet.

_____ **8.** When I am offered snacks or desserts, I decline if I've already had enough sweets or fats.

_____ **9.** I take responsibility for the food choices I make.

_____ **10.** I make good nutrition part of a balanced, healthy life.

Score yourself: Give yourself 3 points for each *always* answer, 1 point for each *sometimes*, and 0 for each *never*. Write your score here _____.

26 to 30 points: Excellent—You understand the importance of nutrition to your health.

21 to 25 points: Good—You often make healthy eating decisions.

16 to 20 points: Fair—You've made a good start, but you can put your nutritional knowledge to better use.

Under 16 points: You need to work harder on having healthy eating habits.

Name _____ Class _____ Date _____

Health Behavior Contract

Nutrition

My Goals: I, _____, will accomplish one or more of the following goals:

I will improve my overall nutrition.

I will follow the Dietary Guidelines for Americans.

I will make healthy food choices at every meal.

Other: _____

_____

My Reasons: By improving my nutrition, I will improve my overall health and feel confident that I am doing something good for my body. I will learn what foods are good for me, and I will be able to make healthy food choices.

Other: _____

_____

My Values: Personal values that will help me meet my goals are

_____

_____

My Plan: The actions I will take to meet my goals are

_____

_____

Evaluation: I will use my Health Journal to keep a log of actions I took to fulfill this contract. After 1 month, I will evaluate my goals. I will adjust my plan if my goals are not being met. If my goals are being met, I will consider setting additional goals.

Signed _____

Date _____

Activity

Life Skills: Assessing Your Health

Lesson: Nutrition and Your Health
ANALYZING YOUR ENERGY NEEDS

You've learned that food does much more than stop hunger. It helps you grow and stay healthy. Food also gives your body energy. How does eating affect your ability to stay active? To find out, keep an energy diary.

For three days, keep track of how much energy you have just before and about a half hour after each meal and snack. Ask yourself if you had more energy, less energy, or felt the same after eating. Pick school days for the first two days of your diary, and and let the third day be a weekend day. When you've finished your diary, review your findings and answer these questions.

1. Did you notice having more energy after eating?

_____

_____

_____

2. Did the kinds of food you ate make a difference in how much energy you had?

_____

_____

_____

3. Were there times when you ate because your energy was low? Did it help?

_____

_____

_____

4. Would you change anything about the times you eat or the kinds of food you eat, based on your diary?

_____

_____

_____

_____

Activity

Life Skills: Being a Wise Consumer

Lesson: Eating for Life
USING NUTRITION INFORMATION SOURCES

Imaging that you and your mother go to the supermarket. Your mother says you can pick the foods she'll purchase for you for the week, "as long as you make healthy choices." As you go through the store, you realize that you have decisions to make in each food aisle.

Read the following situations. After each, write down which information source would help you to make healthy nutrition decisions. Write *P* if you would use the MyPyramid food guidance system, *N* for the Nutrition Facts label, or *D* for the Dietary Guidelines for Americans.

_____ **1. Your mother asks you, "How do I know you understand what good nutrition is?"** Which food guide best helps you answer her?

_____ **2. The first part of the store sells fruits and vegetables.** How much of each of these groups will you need for the week?

_____ **3. The next aisle sells two varieties of spaghetti sauce.** Your mother suggests, "Pick the one with fewer calories."

_____ **4. Your next stop is the dairy case.** There are four kinds of milk: whole, skim, 1 percent, and 2 percent. Your mother suggests picking the one with the lowest amount of fat.

_____ **5. Your next stop is the meat and fish corner.** There are rows of packages containing ground beef, pork, chicken, and other meats and fish. "Well," your mother says, "how much should we buy?"

_____ **6. Your mother then asks you what kind of meat you want to buy.** Remember that some meats have a lot of fat.

_____ **7. You're now in the canned food sections.** As you look at the canned foods, you notice many are very high in sodium.

_____ **8. Your mother tells you to finish up with your shopping soon and that you have time for one last aisle.** There are three food aisles that you have not visited. One has candy and snack foods, one has water and soft drinks, and the third has pasta and rice. Which aisle do you choose?

Skills Worksheet

Concept Review

Lesson: Facts About Drugs

_____ **1.** Which factor can affect a person's reaction to a drug?
  a. the amount of drug he or she consumes
  b. how much he or she weighs
  c. how much food is in his or her stomach
  d. All of the above

2. Explain why food and water are not drugs.

_____

_____

_____

3. Can you predict how drugs will affect a person? Explain.

_____

_____

_____

Lesson: Medicine

4. Define *medicine*.

_____

_____

_____

5. How can you use medicines safely?

_____

_____

_____

6. Explain the difference between over-the-counter and prescription medicines.

_____

_____

_____

| Concept Review *continued*

7. Explain what side effects are.

_____

_____

_____

8. What information can be found on an OTC medicine label?

_____

_____

_____

9. List three ways to use medicines safely.

_____

_____

_____

_____

Lesson: Illegal Drugs

Match each definition with the correct term. Write the letter in the space provided.

_____**10.** a drug that slows the body down

_____**11.** a drug that speeds up body functions

_____**12.** one of the most commonly used illegal drugs

_____**13.** chemical product that has strong fumes or odors

_____**14.** a drug that introduces people to drug use and increases the risk that they will try other drugs whose effects are stronger

_____**15.** a drug that is abused to build muscle

_____**16.** a drug that can make people see and hear things that do not exist

_____**17.** a drug made from poppy flowers

a. marijuana

b. gateway drug

c. inhalant

d. anabolic steroid

e. stimulant

f. depressant

g. opiate

h. hallucinogen

| Concept Review *continued*

Lesson: Drug Abuse

18. Explain the difference between misuse and abuse.

_____

_____

_____

19. Name some social costs of abusing drugs.

_____

_____

_____

20. Explain how drug abuse affects decisions.

_____

_____

_____

Lesson: Drug Addiction

Write the letter of the correct answer in the space provided.

_____**21.** When a person cannot feel the original effects of a drug when taking the original amount of the drug, he or she has developed a
    a. drug addiction.
    b. withdrawal.
    c. tolerance.
    d. dependence.

_____**22.** Needing a drug in order to feel normal is part of
    a. drug addiction.
    b. withdrawal.
    c. tolerance.
    d. dependence.

_____**23.** The body's reaction to not having a drug that is usually present in the body is called
    a. drug addiction.
    b. withdrawal.
    c. tolerance.
    d. dependence.

Name _____ Class _____ Date _____

| Concept Review *continued*

_____**24.** The failure to control one's use of a drug is called
  a. drug addiction.
  b. withdrawal.
  c. tolerance.
  d. dependence.

25. Explain why recovering from a drug addiction is difficult.

_____

_____

_____

Lesson: Refuse to Abuse

26. What can you do if someone invites you to a party where drugs may be used?

_____

_____

_____

27. How can you find ways to cope without drugs?

_____

_____

_____

28. Why is it important to think about ways to refuse drugs before they are offered to you?

_____

_____

_____

29. How can friends help you avoid drugs?

_____

_____

_____

_____

Name _____ Class _____ Date _____

Health Inventory

Resisting Peer Pressure

Here is a checklist about drugs. Put a check next to each statement that describes you.

_____ **1.** I know that drugs are unpredictable.

_____ **2.** I read the labels on over-the-counter medications carefully before taking them.

_____ **3.** I read the labels on prescription medications carefully before taking them.

_____ **4.** I avoid situations in which I might be offered illegal drugs.

_____ **5.** I know that using inhalants can have serious consequences for my health and can even cause death.

_____ **6.** I know that using anabolic steroids is not a healthy way to build muscle.

_____ **7.** I know I risk making unhealthy decisions if I use drugs.

_____ **8.** I know the signs of drug addiction and know where to go for help if I think someone has a problem.

_____ **9.** I can think of many fun things to do that don't involve drugs.

_____ **10.** I know that the best way to avoid drug addiction is to never start abusing drugs.

Give yourself one point for each checkmark. Write your score here _____.

7–10 points: Excellent—You know the facts about drugs.
4–6 points: Good—You know some of the facts, but you should know more.
Under 4 points: Poor—You would benefit from learning more about drugs.

Name _____ Class _____ Date _____

Health Behavior Contract

Understanding Drugs

My Goals: I, _____, will accomplish one or more of the following goals:

I will stay drug free.

I will know where to get help if a friend or I ever need help dealing with a drug problem.

I will use refusal skills if drugs are offered to me.

Other: _____

_____

My Reasons: By staying drug free, using refusal skills, and being prepared to deal with drug-related problems, I will be promoting my health and safety. Being drug free will allow me to pursue my interests, maintain relationships, and reach other goals.

Other: _____

_____

My Values: Personal values that will help me meet my goals are

_____

_____

_____

My Plan: The actions I will take to meet my goals are

_____

_____

_____

Evaluation: I will use my Health Journal to keep a log of actions I took to fulfill this contract. After 1 month, I will evaluate my goals. I will adjust my plan if my goals are not being met. If my goals are being met, I will consider setting additional goals.

Signed _____

Date _____

Name _____ Class _____ Date _____

Life Skills: Being a Wise Consumer

Lesson: Medicine

THE IMPORTANCE OF MEDICINE LABELS

Read the following situation. Then, answer the questions.

You have a really bad headache, so you get an over-the-counter pain medicine. You read the label and take two pills. Two hours later, your head is still hurting. You look at the medicine label again. It says to take one to two pills every four to six hours. Your head is really hurting.

1. What should you do before taking any over-the-counter medicine?

_____

_____

_____

2. Should you take another pill before the recommended time? Explain your answer.

_____

_____

_____

3. Why is it important to carefully read the labels on over-the-counter drugs?

_____

_____

_____

4. If your headache gets worse and does not go away, what can you do?

_____

_____

_____

_____

Activity

Life Skills: Coping

Lesson: Drug Addiction
DEALING WITH STRESS

Read the following situation. Then, answer the questions.

You are having a really bad week. You failed a test and you got in a huge fight with your best friend. Another friend, Ryan, notices you are down. He says he has just the solution to your problems. He offers you a marijuana joint. Ryan tells you it will make you relax, feel good, and forget all of your problems. He tells you he smokes it every day.

1. Why might you want to take the joint?

_____

_____

_____

_____

2. Should you take the joint to feel better?

_____

_____

_____

_____

3. What could happen if you do decide to smoke the joint?

_____

_____

_____

_____

4. List some other ways you can cope with your problems besides turning to drugs.

_____

_____

_____

_____

Skills Worksheet

Concept Review

Lesson: Tobacco and Alcohol as Drugs

_____ 1. What factors can affect how a person will react to drinking alcohol?
   a. how much alcohol they have consumed in the past
   b. how much they weigh
   c. how much food is in their stomach
   d. All of the above

2. Explain why tobacco and alcohol are drugs.

   _____

   _____

   _____

3. Explain why people's reactions to tobacco and alcohol are unpredictable.

   _____

   _____

   _____

Lesson: Tobacco Products

4. What effect does carbon monoxide have on the body?

   _____

   _____

5. Explain the physical effects of tar.

   _____

   _____

   _____

6. List the early effects of smoking cigarettes.

   _____

   _____

   _____

| Concept Review *continued*

Match each item in the right column to the correct term in the left column.

_____ **7.** a dangerous chemical found in all tobacco products

_____ **8.** a disease in which the lungs are so damaged that they cannot absorb enough oxygen

_____ **9.** a mixture of exhaled smoke and smoke from the ends of cigarettes

_____ **10.** a disease in which abnormal cells destroy healthy body tissues

_____ **11.** a product made from chopped tobacco leaves that can be tucked under the lips

_____ **12.** powdered tobacco that can be sniffed

a. ETS

b. nicotine

c. snuff

d. chewing tobacco

e. emphysema

f. cancer

Lesson: Alcohol

13. List three possible effects of intoxication.

_____

_____

_____

14. The percentage of alcohol in a person's blood is called the

_____ .

15. Name two health problems caused by long-term alcohol abuse.

_____

_____

16. Explain how alcohol can impair the ability of a person to drive.

_____

_____

17. What are two characteristics of babies born with fetal alcohol syndrome?

_____

_____

Lesson: Addiction

_____**18.** The body's ability to resist the effects of a drug is called
   a. drug addiction.
   b. alcoholism.
   c. tolerance.
   d. None of the above

_____**19.** Needing a drug in order to feel normal is part of
   a. drug addiction.
   b. alcoholism.
   c. tolerance.
   d. None of the above

_____**20.** A disease caused by physical and psychological dependence on alcohol is called
   a. drug addiction.
   b. alcoholism.
   c. tolerance.
   d. None of the above

21. Explain how alcoholism can affect the family of a person who has alcoholism.

_____

_____

_____

22. Name three support programs for people who have alcoholism and for their families.

_____

_____

_____

23. Explain why it is difficult to quit using drugs once a person is addicted.

_____

_____

_____

_____

_____

| Concept Review *continued*

Lesson: Feeling Pressure

24. Describe how each group of people can pressure teens to try tobacco and alcohol:

friends:

_____

_____

family:

_____

_____

role models:

_____

_____

25. Explain how peer pressure can be positive or negative.

_____

_____

26. How does the media pressure teens to use tobacco and alcohol?

_____

_____

_____

Lesson: Refusing Tobacco and Alcohol

27. Describe two ways you can refuse tobacco or alcohol.

_____

_____

28. List three drug-free ways to be social.

_____

_____

_____

Name _____ Class _____ Date _____

Activity

Health Inventory

Resisting Peer Pressure

Read each of the following statements about peer pressure. Then, put a checkmark next to each statement that describes your behavior.

_____ 1. If a friend were smoking a cigarette and offered me one, I would accept and smoke the cigarette.

_____ 2. If I were with a group of other people who were smoking, I would smoke too, just to fit in.

_____ 3. If a friend were drinking a beer and offered me one, I would accept and drink it.

_____ 4. If I were at a social gathering where most people were drinking alcohol, I would drink too.

_____ 5. When I see celebrities smoking, I want to smoke, too.

_____ 6. When I see celebrities drinking alcohol, I want to drink alcohol, too.

_____ 7. If someone who had been drinking offered me a ride home, I would accept so that I wouldn't offend him or her.

_____ 8. I have difficulty resisting peer pressure when faced with difficult decisions.

Give yourself one point for each checkmark. Write your score here _____.

0:     You are good at resisting peer pressure.

1–2: You may be able to resist peer pressure sometimes, but you could work to resist it more consistently.

3–4: You should practice strategies for resisting peer pressure.

More than 4: You know few strategies for resisting peer pressure. You may want to talk to a trusted adult about how to make better decisions for yourself.

Name _____ Class _____ Date _____

Health Behavior Contract

Tobacco and Alcohol

My Goals: I, _____, will accomplish one or more of the following goals:

I will not use tobacco or alcohol.

I will find out where to go for help if a friend suffers from alcoholism.

I will use refusal skills if alcohol and tobacco are offered to me.

Other: _____

_____

My Reasons: By abstaining from tobacco and alcohol and using refusal skills if someone offers tobacco or alcohol to me, I will protect my health. By knowing how to deal with alcoholism, I will be prepared to help my friends and family.

Other: _____

_____

My Values: Personal values that will help me meet my goals are

_____

_____

_____

My Plan: The actions I will take to meet my goals are

_____

_____

_____

Evaluation: I will use my Health Journal to keep a log of actions I took to fulfill this contract. After 1 month, I will evaluate my goals. I will adjust my plan if my goals are not being met. If my goals are being met, I will consider setting additional goals.

Signed _____

Date _____

Name _____ Class _____ Date _____

Life Skills: Communicating Effectively

Lesson: Addiction
COMMUNICATING WITH FRIENDS
Read the following situation. Then answer the questions.

Your friend Nora has been drinking a lot of alcohol for the past few months. You used to do things with her on the weekends, but now all she does is go to parties where alcohol is served. You went with her once and felt very uncomfortable because she was intoxicated and acting totally out of control. Nora sneaks some of her parents' alcohol every day and brings it to school. She goes to her locker several times a day to sneak a drink. You've asked Nora why she's doing this, and she told you it makes her feel good—she even said she drinks by herself when she's home alone. She can't even go one day without having a drink now.

1. Does Nora have a problem with alcohol? Explain your answer.

_____

_____

_____

2. How could you communicate your concerns to Nora?

_____

_____

_____

3. Where could you suggest Nora go for support and to get help with her problem?

_____

_____

_____

4. If Nora will not get help on her own, to whom will you go with your concerns?

_____

_____

_____

_____

Name _____ Class _____ Date _____

Life Skills: Evaluating Media Messages

Lesson: Feeling Pressure
ADVERTISING ALCOHOL AND TOBACCO
Find several magazines that contain advertisements for alcohol and tobacco products.

1. Which magazines did you find?

   _____

   _____

   _____

2. Who typically reads each magazine?

   _____

   _____

   _____

3. Describe some of the ads for alcohol. How do the ads portray people who drink alcohol?

   _____

   _____

   _____

4. Describe some of the ads for tobacco products. How do the ads portray people who use tobacco products?

   _____

   _____

   _____

5. Explain how these images compare to the real effects of using alcohol and tobacco products.

   _____

   _____

   _____

   _____

Skills Worksheet

Concept Review

Lesson: Safety Around Home

1. Describe three accidents that happen at home.

_____

_____

_____

_____ **2.** Which of the following is NOT a way to stay safe in a vehicle?
   a. Wear your seat belt.
   b. Put young children in a safety seat.
   c. Put children younger than 12 in the back seat.
   d. Distract the driver.

3. Describe five ways to stay safe when you cycle or skate.

_____

_____

_____

_____

_____

4. A _____ is an alarm that detects smoke from a fire.

5. A _____ releases chemicals to put out a fire.

Lesson: Safety at School

6. List five causes of violence.

_____

_____

_____

7. Using physical force to hurt someone or cause damage is called

_____.

8. A _____ is a group of people who often use violence.

| Concept Review *continued* | Health and Your Safety |

9. List four ways to avoid violence in school.

_____

_____

_____

_____

Lesson: Seven Ways to Protect Yourself

10. List the seven safety rules and describe how they can protect you from accidental injury.

_____

_____

_____

_____

_____

_____

_____

_____

Lesson: Safety in the Water

11. Explain why you should wear a life jacket while boating.

_____

_____

_____

12. List seven ways to stay safe while swimming.

_____

_____

_____

_____

| Concept Review *continued*

Write the letter of the correct answer in the space provided.

_____ **13.** Which of the following is NOT a good way to avoid drowning?
   a. swimming alone
   b. obeying warning signs
   c. wearing a life jacket
   d. swimming near a lifeguard

_____ **14.** Which is NOT a good way to save a drowning person?
   a. call for help
   b. jump into the water
   c. throw a life preserver
   d. All of the above

15. How should you get into an unfamiliar body of water?

_____

_____

16. What technique can you use if you are too tired to keep swimming?

_____

_____

Lesson: Weather Emergencies and Natural Disasters

Match each item in the right column to the correct term in the left column. Write the letter in the space provided.

_____ **17.** overflowing of water into areas that are normally dry

_____ **18.** spinning column of air that has high wind speeds and touches the ground

_____ **19.** large, spinning tropical weather system that has wind speeds of at least 74 miles per hour

_____ **20.** natural event that causes widespread injury, death, and property damage

_____ **21.** shaking of the Earth's surface caused by movement along a break in the Earth's crust

_____ **22.** heavy rainstorm with strong winds, lightning, and thunder

a. natural disaster

b. thunderstorm

c. tornado

d. hurricane

e. flood

f. earthquake

| Concept Review *continued*

23. List three ways to learn about weather emergencies.

_____

_____

_____

Lesson: Dealing with Emergencies

24. Emergency medical care for someone who has been hurt or who is sick is

called _____.

25. Describe when you should give first aid.

_____

_____

_____

26. List five things you should tell an operator during an emergency phone call.

_____

_____

_____

_____

_____

Lesson: Giving First Aid

27. Explain how to give abdominal thrusts to an adult.

_____

_____

_____

_____

_____

28. An emergency technique in which a rescuer gives air to someone who is not

breathing is called _____.

| Concept Review *continued*

29. Describe how to treat a victim of poisoning.

_____

_____

_____

_____

_____

_____

30. Describe how to treat wounds.

_____

_____

_____

_____

_____

_____

_____

31. List and describe the three types of burns.

_____

_____

_____

_____

_____

_____

_____

Activity

Health Inventory

Home Safety Checklist

Here is a questionnaire about home safety. Put a check next to each statement that applies to your home.

_____ **1.** I leave objects on the stairs.

_____ **2.** I leave objects lying on the floor.

_____ **3.** I often forget to wipe up spills.

_____ **4.** I stand on a chair to get to things I can't reach.

_____ **5.** I often burn candles and forget to blow them out when I leave the room.

_____ **6.** There are some frayed electrical cords lying around.

_____ **7.** Power outlets are overloaded.

_____ **8.** There is not a smoke detector in every room.

_____ **9.** I'm not sure where the fire extinguisher is.

_____ **10.** I keep my blow-dryer right next to the bathtub or sink.

_____ **11.** Power outlets are uncovered.

_____ **12.** Sometimes I forget to turn off the stove after I cook something.

Give yourself one point for each checkmark. Write your score here _____.

0–1: Your family is taking the precautions necessary to stay safe.

2–3: Overall, you family is taking safety precautions, but there is some room for improvement.

4–5: Your family could take steps to improve the safety of your home.

More than 5: You may have many dangerous situations in your home. Make a plan with your family to prevent potential accidents.

Name _____ Class _____ Date _____

Health Behavior Contract

Health and Your Safety

My Goals: I, _____, will accomplish one or more of the following goals:

I will avoid violence.

I will make my house safer.

I will be safer around water.

Other: _____

_____

My Reasons: I can keep falls, fires, and electrical shock from happening by paying attention, thinking before I act, knowing my limits, using refusal skills, using safety equipment, changing risky habits, and avoiding risky situations.

Other: _____

_____

My Values: Personal values that will help me meet my goals are

_____

_____

_____

My Plan: The actions I will take to meet my goals are

_____

_____

_____

Evaluation: I will use my Health Journal to keep a log of actions I took to fulfill this contract. After 1 month, I will evaluate my goals. I will adjust my plan if my goals are not being met. If my goals are being met, I will consider setting additional goals.

Signed _____

Date _____

Name _____ Class _____ Date _____

Life Skills: Assessing Your Health

Lesson: Safety Around Home
CHECKING SMOKE DETECTORS AT HOME

Do a smoke detector check of your home. Check to make sure all of your smoke detectors have good batteries and are working properly.

1. How many rooms are in your home?

_____

2. How many smoke detectors are in your home?

_____

3. How many smoke detectors should you have in your home?

_____

4. How can a smoke detector help you in case of a fire?

_____

_____

_____

_____

5. Why is it important to have a smoke detector in every room of your home?

_____

_____

_____

_____

6. How often should you check your smoke detectors to make sure they are working properly?

_____

_____

_____

_____

Name _____ Class _____ Date _____

Life Skills: Coping

Lesson: Dealing with Emergencies
HANDLING AN EMERGENCY AT HOME

Imagine that you are at home alone when the smoke detector goes off. You notice smoke coming from the upstairs area of your home.

1. What should you do first?

_____

_____

2. Where could you go to call for help?

_____

_____

3. What number should you dial to get help?

_____

4. What information should you give the operator when you make the emergency phone call?

_____

_____

_____

5. When should you hang up the phone?

_____

_____

6. What would you do if someone else was in the house with you?

_____

_____

_____